ON YOUR OWN

ON YOUR OWN

Writing Process

BEVERLY CHIN

CAMBRIDGE Adult Education
Prentice Hall Regents, Englewood Cliffs, NJ 07632

Library of Congress Cataloging-in-Publication Data

CHIN, BEVERLY ANN.
    On your own : Writing process / by Beverly Chin.
    ISBN 0-13-634080-6
    1. English language—Rhetoric.   I. Title.
PE1408.C468   1989
808'.042—dc20
                                              89-2233
                                                CIP

Editorial/production supervision and interior design: TUNDE A. DEWEY
Cover design: BEN SANTORA
Manufacturing buyer: MIKE WOERNER

Cover art: George Inness, "Peace and Plenty." The Metropolitan Museum of Art,
    Gift of George A. Hearn, 1894. (94.27)

 © 1990 by Prentice-Hall, Inc.
A Division of Simon & Schuster
Englewood Cliffs, New Jersey 07632

Printed in the United States of America
10 9 8 7 6 5 4 3 2 1

ISBN   0-13-634080-6

Prentice-Hall International (UK) Limited, *London*
Prentice-Hall of Australia Pty. Limited, *Sydney*
Prentice-Hall Canada Inc., *Toronto*
Prentice-Hall Hispanomericana, S.A., *Mexico*
Prentice-Hall of India Private Limited, *New Delhi*
Prentice-Hall of Japan, Inc., *Tokyo*
Prentice-Hall Simon & Schuster Asia Pte. Ltd., *Singapore*
Editora Prentice-Hall do Brasil. Ltda., *Rio de Janeiro*

ACKNOWLEDGMENTS

Executive Editor

James W. Brown

Senior Editor

Robert McIlwaine

Writing Process Editor

Constance V. Mersel

Writing Consultants

Marjorie Jacobs
Adult Education Specialist/Teacher Trainer
Community Learning Center
Cambridge, Massachusetts

Connie Ackerman
Consultant
Adult Basic Education
Ohio Department of Education

Video Consultants

Roger Wyatt
Professor, School of Library Information Management
University of Kansas
Emporia, Kansas

Joan Giummo
Staff Development Media Projects Facilitator
New York City Board of Education

Carol Chiani
Video Computer Animation Workshop
New York, New York

Jim Lyle
Video Publishers, Inc.
New York, New York

Contents

UNIT 3   REVISING FOR STYLE   119

UNIT 4   EDITING AND SHARING   185

INTRODUCTION

On Your Own is the product of over three years' cooperative work by practitioners, consultants, authors, editors and video producers in the field of adult education. In 1986, recognizing the need for a video series at the Pre-GED level, Cambridge undertook to develop this new program, in cooperation with Penn State University's Center for Instructional Design and Interactive Video, its Institute for the Study of Adult Literacy, its public television station WPSX TV and its College of Education.

On Your Own has been shaped throughout its development by the demands of the 1988 GED exam, with its emphasis on writing skills and on problem-solving, and by the concern for adult literacy in the American workforce. The situations in the video dramas were scripted to show adult learners applying basic skills to solve practical problems as consumers, citizens and employees. Both motivational and instructional, *On Your Own* was thoroughly reviewed by consultants, teachers and administrators to make sure the video dramas dealt with real-life tasks and modeled the application of skills in clear, carefully paced examples. The same process ensured that the texts were written to a seventh to ninth grade reading level, with minimum terminology, survival-skills content and many exercises.

The design of the program, in which short video dramas lead into the extended work in the texts, was endorsed by an initial survey of over thirty leading educators in adult education. Samples of both videos and texts were shown to focus groups in every region of the country, and have been field-tested by the Appalachian Youth Service, by a worksite literacy program of the Alcoa Corporation, and by several urban and rural learning programs supervised by the nationally known adult literacy consultant, Ms. Nancy Woods.

The result is a series of interacting videos and videotexts which is designed for flexible use by students and teachers in the many different settings of adult education: a teacher with a class of one subject; semi-independent work to "free up" the teacher; TV room viewing of several strands before work in the texts by small groups; individual study in labs, or at home with a TV/VCR. The videos can be played before or after work in the texts for motivation or review or both, and the texts can be used apart from the videos as a complete Pre-GED series at the seventh to ninth grade, reading level. *On Your Own* is an immediately valuable teaching tool for programs in worksites, libraries and correctional institutions, and is adaptable for competency-based and ESL instruction.

Cambridge is pleased to offer this versatile, state-of-the-art video series as a new learning resource for adult education. As throughout its development, we welcome comments and questions from practitioners about its design and content, as well as reports on its varied applications by teachers and adult learners.

About the Author

Dr. Beverly Chin, the author of *On Your Own: Writing Process*, is Professor of English in the English Department of the University of Montana and Director of the Montana Writing Project. A nationally known consultant on writing process, she has conducted scores of teacher-training seminars for educators in high schools, colleges and adult learning centers across the country. Particularly interested in the use of media in connection with writing, she contributed significantly to the instructional portions of the video scripts. Dr. Chin is also the author of *On Your Own: Grammar,* which is designed to complement the writing process text in the series.

TO THE STUDENT

What Is This Book About?

This book is about writing. It will teach you how to write down what you know so that other people can understand your thoughts. You will find that writing is useful at work, at home, in school, and in a variety of personal situations.

Each chapter tells you something new about writing. The exercises give you opportunities to write. The checklist helps you think about your own writing with the help of another person. Discussing your ideas with other people is an important part of writing. Discussion helps you get ideas, organize them, and write sentences that are clear and interesting.

The *Video Focus* section tells you what to pay attention to when you watch the video. The video shows how the writing skills you learn in the chapter are used in real life. The *Video Replay* section gives you a chance to review the video writing activity and write about similar topics after you have practiced the writing skills in the chapter. It may also give you more ideas for writing.

What is Writing?

Like talking, writing is a way of communicating information, ideas, and feelings to other people. For example, when you fill out a job application, you communicate information that tells an employer why you should be hired. When you write to your neighbors about helping with a block clean-up, you communicate feelings of pride in your neighborhood and ideas for improving it.

Writing is often done with the help or participation of other people. They let us know how fully we are communicating our thoughts.

Sometimes writing is very simple. For example, if you have to run an errand when you are expecting friends to visit, you might leave them a message on the door. You think about what you need to say, organize the ideas, and write this.

Please wait for me. I had to go to the store and will be back in ten minutes.

Sometimes, though, writing requires more planning and organizing. If you were writing a letter to your employer, you would probably spend more time thinking about your ideas and organizing them. You would want to use the best words to communicate your concerns. You might ask a few coworkers to comment on the letter before you give it to your employer.

When you plan, organize, and write your ideas, you are using the writing process. If you do a good job, you can expect your readers to understand your message.

A process is a series of actions that lead to a result. For example, when you fix up a new house or apartment, you go through a process like this.

1. choosing and buying furniture
2. getting the furniture delivered
3. arranging the furniture in various ways until you find one that feels right
4. cleaning and dusting
5. inviting people over for a housewarming party

The result is a comfortable home.

Writing is also a process. The result is that other people learn what you think about a particular topic. The writing process consists of five stages:

1. *Prewriting*

   You select or are given a topic to write about. You think about your audience, or who will read your writing. You also consider your writing purpose—what you want to accomplish with your writing. After you brainstorm, or think up as many ideas as you can, you decide which ideas can be kept and which ones should be discarded.

2. *Drafting*

   You quickly write a paragraph on the topic. This is called the rough draft because you can improve the ideas, organization, sentences, and words later. At this stage, correct spelling, punctuation, and grammar are not important.

3. *Revising*

   You "rethink," or "resee," the writing. You improve the ideas and organization of the rough draft and make the sentences clearer and more interesting.

4. *Editing*

   You check for correct spelling, punctuation, and grammar, and make sure the sentences are complete.

5. *Sharing*

   You copy the draft to include all changes made through revising and editing. Then you share the paragraph with one or more people—your audience. If you have followed all the stages of the writing process, the audience should be able to understand your written message. You can take pride in communicating clearly.

For very short pieces of writing such as the note about the visit above, some stages may be left out. However, a paragraph of several sentences is easier to write if all stages are included.

Some stages may take more time to complete than others. Don't worry if this happens to you. Relax, be patient, and enjoy each stage. Remember that the goal of writing is to communicate your ideas to your audience. If you can talk, you can write. And the more often you write, the more comfortable you will feel about writing.

ON YOUR OWN
WRITING PROCESS

UNIT 1

PREWRITING

WHAT IS PREWRITING?

Prewriting is what you do to get ready for actually writing a letter, report, or petition. When you read a well-written paragraph, you may have the impression that it was written with little effort. You may believe that good writers write easily. In fact, good writers do a lot of thinking before they even start writing—they do prewriting.

- They have to decide on a topic—exactly what they will be writing about. Sometimes, like the writers in the videos you will watch, they will know right away what they want to write about. Their writing topic is obvious because they have a practical problem that makes them want to write about it. At other times, writers are asked to write about any topic, and have to choose one.
- They must choose an audience—the person or group of people that would be most interested in what they have to say about this topic.
- They need to think about what their writing purpose is. With this topic are they planning to tell a story? Explain how to do something? Describe where something is or how it looks? Persuade the audience to agree with an opinion?
- They have to gather ideas about their topic.
- They have to write a topic sentence which states the main idea of the paragraph they want to write.
- Writers then go through two more steps before they start writing.

  1. First, they review all the ideas they have gathered on the topic and check to see if they relate to the topic sentence. Are there enough ideas? If not, they add more ideas.
  2. Second, are there any ideas that do not belong in the paragraph? If so, these are discarded.

- Now writers are ready to write a rough draft. A rough draft is not supposed to be perfect, completed writing. It is a first try—a quickly written, rough version of the piece of writing. This rough draft is like a pencil sketch that artists make before they start work on an oil painting. The sketch gives them an idea of how the finished piece will look.

ON YOUR OWN

2:30   2

Choosing Writing Purpose and Audience

VIDEO FOCUS

The employees of Prime Printing must cross a dangerous highway to get food. They would like their company to install food vending machines and a coffee maker in the employees' lunchroom. After deciding to put their request in writing, they discuss their writing purpose and to whom they should send a letter.

Choosing a suitable **purpose** and **audience** for a piece of writing is an important first step in the writing process.

Chapter Objectives

After seeing the video and completing the chapter, you will understand how to

- choose the audience and purpose for your writing
- distinguish between everyday and businesslike language.

Key Words

Here are some important words that appear in this chapter and on the video. Notice how they are used. If you come across an unfamiliar word that is not on this list, write it down and ask your teacher to explain it to you.

topic	to narrate
writing purpose	to explain
audience	to describe
everyday language	to persuade
businesslike language	

3

Lesson 1 WRITING ABOUT A TOPIC

In the video, the employees of Prime Printing plan to write a letter to the company president. What they are writing about—their topic—is their wish to have vending machines and a coffee maker installed in the employees' lunchroom.

A **topic** is a general idea for a piece of writing or a speech. Most of the time, your topic will be ready-made. You will want to, or be asked to, write about something specific. Here are some examples of ready-made topics and the reasons you might be writing about them:

Topic	*Reason for Writing*
the accident you saw yesterday	you need to make a written accident report to the police
the problems with your elevator	you need to tell your landlord in writing how to fix it
why a company should hire you	you need to write a letter of application to an employer
why a parking lot should not be built next to your house	you need to tell the City Council in writing
what your jacket looked like	you need to report the theft to the police in writing

Lesson 2 KNOWING YOUR WRITING PURPOSE

The way you write about a topic depends on what you want to accomplish with your writing: Do you want **to narrate** (to tell a story)? Do you want **to explain** something? **to describe** something? **to persuade** the reader to agree with you about something? What you want to accomplish in your writing is your **writing purpose**.

You can write about one topic for each of these four different purposes. For example, imagine that you saw an auto accident. The accident would be the topic. You might write this topic for the following purposes:

Writing purpose	*Writer tells*
to narrate	what happened in the accident
to explain	why this intersection has so many accidents
to describe	what the damaged car looked like

| to persuade | why certain changes should be made to prevent accidents here |

Here are examples of each kind of writing.

To Narrate

At 6:15 P.M. on January 6, a car and a van collided at Broadway and 96th Street. A blue Ford on 96th Street moved into the intersection just as the light changed to red. Then a red van, traveling faster than the rest of the traffic on Broadway, hit the Ford on the driver's side. The driver of the Ford was so badly hurt that he would not walk or talk. No one else involved in the accident. Finally, at 6:25 P.M., the police and ambulance arrived.

To Explain

The intersection at Broadway and 96th Street has been dangerous for years. The major reason is that heavy traffic exists from the bridge at 96th Street and backs up for several blocks. Because the green lights for 96th Street are too short and the red lights are too long, drivers become frustrated. Also, some Broadway drivers are unaware of the problem here. As a result, accidents happen.

To Describe

The damage to the blue, 1987 Ford is mostly on the driver's side. The front bumper is bent, and the windshield shattered. The left front fender and the driver's door are destroyed beyond repair. The back passenger door on the left side is off its hinges, and the taillight is broken.

To Persuade

The accident rate at the intersection of Broadway and 96th Street can be reduced. The timing of the lights should be changed so that 96th Street drivers have time to cross Broadway. Signs should alert Broadway drivers to problems at 96th Street. Traffic exiting from the bridge should be directed to more than one street. Until some changes are made, a traffic cop should be present.

To decide what your writing purpose should be, ask yourself what you want to accomplish with your writing. The following definitions will help you identify your writing purpose.

If you want	*Your writing purpose is*
to tell a story	to narrate
to tell how to do something, or why something happened, or why things are the way they are	to explain
to tell about the way something or someone looks; to tell the different characteristics of someone or something	to describe
to tell why the reader should agree with your opinion	to persuade

PRACTICE

Identify the purpose of each topic below by writing **N** (*narrate*), **E** (*explain*), **D** (*describe*), or **P** (*persuade*) in the space beside it.

a. _____ the day I met my spouse

b. _____ how to lose weight

c. _____ why everyone should wear a seat belt

d. _____ the way the bar looked after the fight

e. _____ why children should learn the value of money

f. _____ why I am for birth control

g. _____ how I prepare my favorite dessert

h. _____ how I lost my wallet yesterday

i. _____ how to enroll in GED preparation classes

j. _____ why you should save part of your paycheck

k. _____ what my car looked like after the accident

l. _____ why I am against early marriages

Lesson 3 DECIDING ON YOUR AUDIENCE

The person or group of people who might be interested in reading your writing is your **audience**. Who should be interested in reading about the accident? The *police* and *insurance company* want to know what happened first, second, third, and so on, so they would read the narration. The *insurance company* also wants to know what damage was done to the car, so it would read the description of the way the car looks.

The *City Council* knows this intersection is dangerous, but is not sure why. The council members would read the explanation. Finally, if you want to demand changes, you might write a letter to the editor of the local newspaper. The *newspaper readers* would be the audience for your paragraph of persuasion.

Lesson 4   MAKING YOUR LANGUAGE SUIT THE AUDIENCE

Businesslike language is used when the writer does not know the audience well and wants to make a good impression. The police, the insurance company, and the City Council take care of business and government matters. You probably don't know them or the newspaper readers. Such audiences need information written in **businesslike language**.

On the other hand, friends and relatives are more interested in our personal reactions, so **everyday language** might be more suitable. Here is the same accident written in everyday language:

> Mom, you know how you always say Broadway and 96th Street is an accident waiting to happen? Well, last night, it did! Two cars crashed into each other. Boy, were they in a hurry! One driver got really hurt. Blood was everywhere. I was so upset!

Notice how the ideas and language changed when you wrote to your mother. For the first time, you mention that you were upset. Whether you are writing or talking, how you express yourself partly depends on who your audience is. Let's look at another example of how language changes to suit the audience.

Imagine you are a salesclerk having a busy day. Many customers complain rudely when you tell them that the store has run out of sale items. Several are impatient with the long lines.

You might talk about your day to your supervisor in one way, to a customer in the store in another way, to a coworker in a third way, and to your spouse in a fourth way.

To Your Supervisor

> I'm glad that the special sale is going so well. However, I do think that we need another salesclerk to help all these customers.

Your supervisor is interested in how the sale is going, so you report that it is going well and suggest ways to solve a problem.

To a Customer

> I'm sorry to keep you waiting. Yes, we are out of stock on that item, but I can give you a rain check.

The customer wants to be treated well by the store. You represent the store, so you apologize for the long wait and mention the rain check.

To Your Coworker

> I can't wait to take my next break. My feet are killing me. If one more customer complains about the out-of-stock sales items, I think I'll scream!

Your coworker probably feels the same way you do about the sale. You can express your frustration without being afraid of losing your job.

To Your Spouse

> The next time the store decides to run a sale, I'm taking the day off. I feel as grouchy as all those customers. I wish nobody had ever invented sales and rain checks.

Your spouse cares about how you feel, so you can count on his or her sympathy and talk freely about your troubles on the job. The same words might make your supervisor wonder if you will come to work on another sale day.

The topic in all cases is dealing with customers during a sale. However, from this topic came four different ideas—improving the situation (supervisor), helping others to cope with it (customers), complaining about it (coworkers), and wishing it away (spouse). Knowing your audience helps you decide what information to include.

The language also changed according to who the listener was. The language of the first two examples was businesslike. You wanted to make a good impression on your supervisor, and you did not know the customer. The last two examples were written in everyday language, which is suited to friends and family. You use businesslike language for someone you are not close to personally. You use everyday language for people you know well.

Remember to think about your relationship to your audience when you are deciding what kind of language to use.

Read each of the following paragraphs. For each paragraph, decide on the appropriate audience for it and whether the *language* used is *businesslike* or *everyday*.

1. I am returning the toaster. The pop-up mechanism does not work properly. It throws the toast onto the floor when the toast is done. The warranty is still in effect. Please fix the toaster or give me a new one. Thank you.

The audience is

a. _____ a repair shop

b. _____ the store where you bought the toaster

c. _____ the friend who gave you the toaster

The language is

a. _____ businesslike

b. _____ everyday

2. Guess what! My new toaster has decided to fling the toast on the floor! I wonder if I could train it to flip the toast directly into the garbage, since that is where it ends up. Making breakfast is a lot of laughs, but I'm still hungry in the end.

The audience is

a. _____ a repair shop

b. _____ a friend

c. _____ the manufacturer

The language is

a. _____ businesslike

b. _____ everyday

3. We need a low-cost day care center at the factory. Many of us have young children. However, we cannot afford outside childcare fees. Even if we could, few services are open before 8:00 A.M. Our shift begins at 7 A.M. All of us would be more productive if we weren't worried about our children's welfare.

The audience is

a. _____ your best friend

b. _____ the factory manager

c. _____ your mother

The language is

a. _____ businesslike

b. _____ everyday

4. The company should put a day care center in the factory. If I don't find some cheap or free way to take care of the kids while I'm working, I'll probably have to quit my job. What lousy luck! I was just beginning to be able to pay my brother back the money he lent me last year. It felt great to be on my own.

The audience is

a. _____ your best friend
b. _____ the factory manager
c. _____ the company president

The language is

a. _____ businesslike
b. _____ everyday

REVIEW EXERCISE

Choose a *topic* from the following list. Decide on your *writing purpose, audience,* and kind of *language.* Write the information in the spaces provided.

_____ how to take care of your teeth
_____ why drinking and driving don't mix
_____ how to fix a leaky faucet
_____ how to shop for bargains
_____ what happened when there was a fire on our block
_____ why people should vote
_____ what happened during the tenants' meeting
_____ how to make a delicious dinner with leftovers
_____ the way I am like my mother (or father)
_____ what my dream house looks like

My topic is _____
My purpose is to _____
My audience is _____
The kind of language I will use is _____

Student Assignment

Choose another topic from the list in the Review Exercise. Decide on your writing purpose, audience, and kind of language. Write the information in the spaces provided.

My topic is _____

My purpose is to _____

My audience is _____

The kind of language I will use is _____

Prewriting Checklist

In the Review Exercise, you chose two topics and decided on the writing purpose, audience, and kind of language for each. Discussing your choices with your teacher or another person can be helpful. Use this checklist as a guide for discussion on each of your topics.

1. What do I want my writing to accomplish?
2. Is my writing purpose appropriate for the audience?
3. Could I talk about my topic with this audience?
4. How might writing about this topic be different than talking about it?

Video Replay

The Prime Printing employees decide against sending their letter to the production manager because she cannot make the final decision about buying new equipment for the lunchroom. Instead, they write to the company president about their request. Write about a situation in which you needed to convince someone to take you seriously.

ON YOUR OWN

CHAPTER **2** *PREWRITING*

Gathering Ideas About a Topic

VIDEO FOCUS

Maria leads her coworkers at Prime Printing in a brainstorming session. They are gathering ideas for their letter to the company president about installing food vending machines and a coffee maker in the employees' lunchroom. Brainstorming with a group of people produces many ideas—sometimes more ideas than one person alone can produce.

Brainstorming is the stage of the writing process when you should have a rush of ideas. You should not judge any of the ideas as good or bad, or worry about the way they are written down. If you want to add to your list of ideas, you may brainstorm more than once.

Working with a partner is often helpful, since someone else may think of things you have not. For instance, can you think of any ideas that Maria and her coworkers left off their brainstorming list that you feel might be added?

Chapter Objectives

After seeing the video and completing the chapter, you will understand how to

- use brainstorming to gather ideas about a topic
- choose and narrow a general topic into a writing topic
- use brainstorming to narrow your topic.

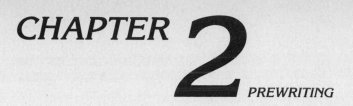

Key Words

Here are some important words that appear in this chapter or on the video. Notice how they are used. If you come across a word that is not on this list, write it down and ask your teacher to explain it to you.

brainstorming
narrowing a topic
clustering

general topic
narrower topic
writing topic

Lesson 1 BRAINSTORMING TO GATHER IDEAS ABOUT A TOPIC

Brainstorming means thinking of as many ideas as you can about your topic and writing them down quickly. When brainstorming, you should not worry about whether the ideas are good or whether the words are spelled correctly. Writing the ideas down as fast as they come to mind is the important thing.

Usually, you will know right away what your topic is, just as Maria and her coworkers know on the video, because you will be writing to get something done in your life. Here is how one group brainstormed on the topic, why the employees' lounge should have a microwave oven.

no way to heat lunches
hot soups/sandwiches better for us
fast ovin—can enjoy breaks/lunch hours more
hotplate takes too long
microwave ovens at home
management should care about workers

No ideas are discarded at this stage. Notice that preceding ideas are expressed in groups of words rather than in sentences. *Ovin* is misspelled. Saying *management should care about workers* might not make a good impression on the person in authority they are writing to. The fact that the workers have *microwave ovens at home* is not related to the topic.

Here is how another group of people brainstormed on the topic, how to stay healthy.

take vitamins
enuf rest
yearly checkup
brush teeth after each meal
run five miles a day

stay away from sik people
wear right clothes for weather
don't get angry

Notice that the ideas were jotted down in short groups of words. Some of these groups are not sentences. *Enuf* and *sik* are misspelled. That is fine for now.

Although some ideas (for example, *brush teeth after every meal* and *don't get angry*) may not be related to the topic, they stay on the list. Any idea that comes to mind, related or not, good or bad, is included at this stage.

You can brainstorm ideas for the topic by yourself, with another person, or with a small group of people such as your classmates. If you are brainstorming for the first time, begin with a ten-minute session on one topic. As you grow comfortable with brainstorming, you can spend more time doing it.

PRACTICE

Choose at least one topic from each of the following lists. *Brainstorm* at least four ideas for the first topic with another person. For the second topic, brainstorm by yourself.

1. why everyone should vote
   the benefits of physical exercise
   legal rights of people who have been arrested
   what can be done to help the homeless
   the characteristics of a good coworker
   how to care for elderly parents (or how to get medical care for
       children)
   what to do if a fire occurs at home
   how to deal with an alcohol or drug abuse problem

2. how I budget my income
   why you should not cheat on your spouse (or boyfriend/girlfriend)
   what I like (dislike) about my job
   what I like (dislike) about being single (married)
   why getting a GED is important to me
   the importance of having safe sex

Topic 1: _____   *Topic 2:* _____

Brainstorming List: Brainstorming List:

1.   1.

2.   2.

3.   3.

4.   4.

Lesson 2   CHOOSING AND NARROWING A TOPIC

In the video, Maria and her coworkers know the topic they want to write about in their letter to their employer. Sometimes, however, you will be asked to choose your topic. You will not know your topic, and will have to think of one.

If you have the opportunity to choose your topic, pick one that really interests you. You are more likely to enjoy writing about something you know. Writers get ideas for topics from their own thoughts, feelings, and experiences. Ideas also can come from other people, television, movies, and printed materials such as magazines, newspapers, and books. Here are some examples of **general topics** you might write about.

proud moments	music	elections
movies	jobs	law
home repairs	childcare	television

Each of these is a good topic, but they are all too big for anyone to write about in an organized way. You always need to choose a specific part of general topic—in other words, to **narrow** it, to create a **narrower topic.** Then, you have to figure out exactly what you want to write about. To do this, you need to choose a still narrower topic, which will be your **writing topic**. Your writing topic is what you know the most about. It is the part of the general topic that you are really interested in writing about. Look at the following examples of general topics, narrower topics, and writing topics.

General Topic	*Narrower Topic*	*My Writing Topic*
proud moments	success at work	the new job I was promoted to at work
home repairs	plumbing repairs	how to fix a leaky faucet

movies	Oscars	who I think should get the Best Actress Award this year
music	rock music	why I like heavy metal rock music
jobs	nursing jobs	the responsibilities of a nurse's aide
childcare	babysitters	babysitting problems of working mothers
elections	local elections	why I will not vote for the mayor this year
law	drug laws	what I think the penalty for drug possession should be
television	favorite TV shows	my favorite character on the "Cosby" show

You can choose different writing topics according to your interests and your writing purpose. You may start with *music* as your topic, narrow it to *rock music,* and decide you want to tell about my *best night at the Hard Rock Cafe.* Your writing purpose would be to narrate, to tell a story. The purpose for the writing topic, *why I like heavy metal rock music,* is to explain. If you narrowed the same general topic to *the differences between heavy metal rock music and new wave music,* your purpose would be to explain or describe some of these differences. You also could narrow music down to *why Michael Jackson is the best rock singer.* With this topic, your purpose would be to persuade. You can narrow your topic by using your own experience, drawing on someone else's experience, or thinking or reading about ideas related to the general topic.

Lesson 3   USING BRAINSTORMING TO NARROW A TOPIC

In the video, and in the first part of this chapter, you saw how brainstorming can be used to produce ideas about a writing topic. You also can use brainstorming to help you choose a specific part of a general topic—to narrow a general topic down to a writing topic. Look at this brainstorming list on the general topic, accidents.

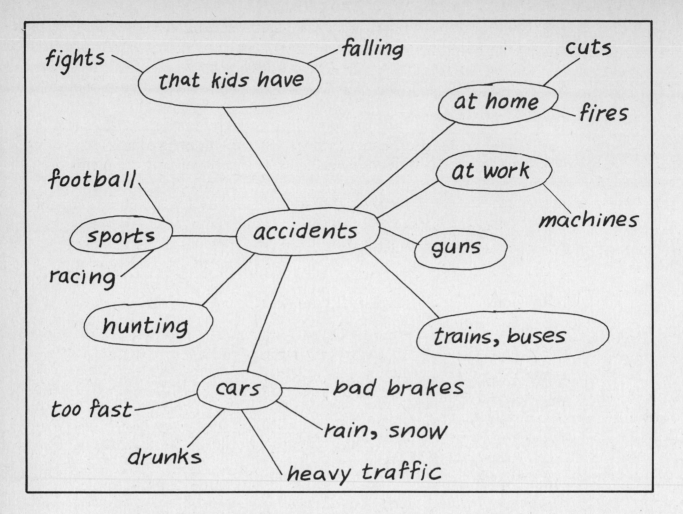

The way this brainstorming list is written is called **clustering**. In clustering, you draw a picture of your brainstorming with the general topic in the center and all the more specific topics coming out of it. You can then draw even more specific topics coming out of the specific ones.

This brainstorming has produced more ideas about *car accidents* than on any other narrower topic. Car accidents is the most interesting narrower topic for this writer. The most interesting ideas about car accidents for the writer are *the causes of car accidents*. Now he or she can choose a writing topic.

    General Topic: accidents
    Narrower Topic: car accidents
    Writing Topic: the causes of the car accidents

Sometimes you choose a writing topic by deciding whether you are for or against something, for example, *the death penalty*. *The death penalty* is a general topic that should be narrowed. A brainstorming list for it might be:

for all murders	treason—spies, selling
child abuse	government secrets
killing a cop	arson—fires causing deaths
killing a president	selling drugs to children
	rape

If you choose *rape* as your narrower topic, you can create your still narrower writing topic by deciding whether you are for or against the death penalty for rape.

General Topic:	the death penalty
Narrower Topic:	the death penalty for rape
Writing Topic:	why I am for (against) the death penalty for rape

Once you have your writing topic, you can use brainstorming to produce ideas about it. In brainstorming (and using clustering, if you want to), you may discover that you are for the death penalty for rape in some cases and not for it in others. Then you might want to change your writing topic to *pros and cons about the death penalty for rape.*

A topic like the death penalty or the death penalty for rape is called an **issue.** Many topics on the essay part of the GED writing test are issue topics. In writing about such topics, your purpose is always to explain (explaining why you believe what you do about the issue) or to persuade (to persuade the reader your beliefs are right).

Lesson 4   NARROWING A TOPIC FOR AN AUDIENCE

When you write for a specific audience, think about its interest when you narrow the topic. In the following example, the writer narrows the general topic, the new neighborhood library, in two different ways for two different audiences. The result is a different narrower topic and writing topic for each audience.

The General Topic:	the new neighborhood library
Audience 1:	party-planning committee for a community group
Interest:	music for a dance contest
Narrower Topic:	tapes of popular music in the new library
Writing Topic:	recent rock tapes you can find in the new library

Audience 2: young married couples expecting children
Interest: educating their children
Narrower Topic: children's material in the new library
Writing Topic: types of children's materials in the new library (books, video and audio tapes, magazines)

PRACTICE

A. Each of the following groups includes a *general topic* and a *narrower topic*. In the blank space in each group, write in a writing topic that you have chosen from the other topics. If you want to, use *brainstorming* or *clustering* to help you find your *writing topic*. The writing topic has been done for the first general topic.

1. **General Topic:** housing
   Narrower Topic: problems of apartment renters
   Writing Topic: *repairs apartment superintendents will not do*

2. **General Topic:** jobs
   Narrower Topic: job interviews
   Writing Topic: _____

3. **General Topic:** death
   Narrower Topic: death of a parent or grandparent
   Writing Topic: _____

4. **General Topic:** employee benefits
   Narrower Topic: health benefits
   Writing Topic: _____

5. **General Topic:** taxes
   Narrower Topic: income taxes
   Writing Topic: _____

6. **General Topic:** movies
   Narrower Topic: movie stars
   Writing Topic: _____

B. In each of the following exercises about *topics* and *audiences*, there is one topic and two different audiences. Each audience has a different interest in the topic. In each exercise, narrow the topic to a writing topic that suits the interests of the audience. Number 1 has been done for you.

1. **General Topic:** fruit   **General Topic:** fruit
   Audience 1: grocers   **Audience 2:** nutrition class
   Interest: low price   **Interest:** health
   Writing Topic: _____   **Writing Topic:** _____

2. **General Topic:** education   **General Topic:** education
   Audience 1: young adults   **Audience 2:** retired adults
   Interest: employment   **Interest:** self-improvement
   Writing Topic: _____   **Writing Topic:** _____

3. **General Topic:** responsibility   **General Topic:** responsibility
   Audience 1: parents   **Audience 2:** teenagers
   Interest: raising children   **Interest:** personal success
   Writing Topic: _____   **Writing Topic:** _____

4. **General Topic:** health   **General Topic:** health
   Audience 1: young mothers   **Audience 2:** older adults
   Interest: healthcare for children   **Interest:** exercise programs
   Writing Topic: _____   **Writing Topic:** _____

5. **General Topic:** discipline   **General Topic:** discipline
   Audience 1: police at a sports event   **Audience 2:** one of sports teams
   Interest: order in the crowd   **Interest:** team discipline for winning
   Writing Topic: _____   **Writing Topic:** _____

6. **General Topic:** work   **General Topic:** work
   Audience 1: supervisors   **Audience 2:** workers
   Interest: worker morale   **Interest:** promotion
   Writing Topic: _____   **Writing Topic:** _____

A. Narrow two of the following topics. Remember that you can use brainstorming to narrow if you wish. You can use what you know from personal experience, reading or thinking, TV, movies, or other people. Try to make the topic as specific as you can. One example has been done for you.

General Topic	*Narrower Topic*	*My Writing Topic*
television	talk shows	*why I like Johnny Carson's "Tonight Show"*
music	_____	_____
addictions	_____	_____
religion	_____	_____
happiness	_____	_____
budgets	_____	_____

B. Choose one writing topic from Review Exercise A and brainstorm three to five ideas.

_____ **Writing Topic:** _____
_____ Brainstorming List:
_____ 1.
_____ 2.
_____ 3.
_____ 4.
_____ 5.

Student Assignment

Choose a general topic of your own and narrow it to a writing topic. Use brainstorming or clustering if you wish. Then brainstorm two or three ideas about your writing topic.

Prewriting Checklist

In Review Exercise A you narrowed topics. In Review Exercise B you brainstormed on a writing topic. Discuss your experience with your teacher or another person. Use this checklist as a guide in your discussion.

1. Did I narrow my general topic to a writing topic?

2. As I narrowed the topic and brainstormed, did I find myself writing down more ideas than I realized I knew?

3. Did I write quickly without worrying whether the ideas were good or were spelled correctly?

4. Did I write without worrying about complete sentences?

Video Replay

Maria's coworkers accept her as a leader. What does she do that encourages other people's trust? What characteristics do you look for in a person when you are deciding to trust that person? Write your responses and share it with another person.

ON YOUR OWN

CHAPTER 3 *PREWRITING*

Creating the Topic Sentence of a Paragraph

VIDEO FOCUS

In the video, Maria and Marge use their brainstorming list to help them write the **topic sentence** of the letter to their employer. The topic sentence tells what the letter will be about, so they work on that first.

It is important to get the reader's attention from the start. One way to do this is to state the topic and the writing purpose in the first sentence, the topic sentence.

Chapter Objectives

After seeing the video and completing the chapter, you will understand how to

- write a topic sentence that tells the audience or reader what the rest of the paragraph will be about
- distinguish between a paragraph and a group of unrelated sentences.

Key Words

Here are some important words that appear in this chapter or on the video. Notice how they are used. If another word appears that you do not understand, write it down and ask your teacher to explain it to you.

main idea	paragraph
support	topic sentence

Lesson 1   WRITING A TOPIC SENTENCE

When Maria and Marge begin to work on their **topic sentence,** they first sort out the **main idea** from the details. The main idea is that the employees want their employer to install a coffee maker and food vending machines in their lunch room. They state this main idea in their topic sentence.

A topic sentence is created from the topic of the writing and the writing purpose. In this single sentence, the writer's message, the main idea of the writing, is directly stated. The topic sentence tells the reader *what* or *who* the paragraph is about.

Suppose you want to write about life insurance. To begin, you would state your topic and writing purpose.

> **Topic:**   why life insurance can be important to many families
>
> **Writing Purpose:**   to explain

Next, you would brainstorm ideas on your topic. Your brainstorming list might include the following ideas:

> provides income if earner dies
> can get loan in emergency
> supplements pensions and Social Security

Next, you would review each idea on the list by asking, "Is this the most important thing I want to say about my topic?" After thinking about the ideas, you might decide that no one idea is more important than any other. However, all ideas relate to the uses of life insurance in various financial institutions. Now you can say to yourself:

> I want to explain that life insurance can be important to many families because it is helpful in various situations.

From this thought, you might write the following topic sentence:

> Life insurance can be important for families because it is helpful in a variety of situations.

The topic sentence most often appears at the beginning of a paragraph. (Skilled writers sometimes place the topic sentence in the middle or at the end of a paragraph.) When the paragraph begins with the topic sentence, the topic and writing purpose are immediately clear both to the writer and the reader.

Write a *topic sentence* for each of the following examples. Your topic sentence should include the topic and writing purpose. Remember that there is more than one way to write a topic sentence. You can arrange the words in the sentence in several ways. The first topic sentence has been written for you.

1. **Topic:** importance of eating a balanced diet
   Writing Purpose: to explain
   Brainstorming List: eat a variety of foods daily
   eat enough of each kind of food
   food has vitamins, minerals,
   and energy prevents disease
   maintains good health
   Topic Sentence: *Eating a balanced diet gives your body the vitamins, minerals, and energy it needs to stay healthy and prevents disease.*

Note: This topic sentence could have been written this way also:

A balanced diet helps you stay healthy and prevents disease by giving your body the vitamins, minerals, and energy it needs.

You also could write it this way:

If you eat a balanced diet, your body will have the vitamins, minerals and energy it needs to stay healthy and avoid disease.

2. **Topic:** the office where I work
   Writing Purpose: to describe
   Brainstorming List: 12 feet wide and 15 feet long
   piles of boxes by front and side walls
   desk and work table facing one door
   work schedule, no pictures on walls
   no windows
   one small lamp on desk—only light
   Topic Sentence: _____

3.   **Topic:** how to paint an apartment
  Writing Purpose: to explain
  Brainstorming List: move all furniture to center of room
        take all pictures off walls
        put drop cloths over everything
        scrape walls, plaster if need to
        prime walls with water or oil if walls bad
          to cover plaster marks
        paint—corners first with brush, open parts
          with roller

  Topic Sentence: _____

4.   **Topic:** why neighborhood residents should partici-
        pate in a renewal plan
  Writing Purpose: to persuade
  Brainstorming List: luxury apartments to replace present
          buildings
        tenants have no place to go
        make needs known to housing authority
        some apartments should be for big families
        elderly on fixed incomes need place to live

  Topic Sentence: _____

5.   **Topic:** dividing up the housework on Saturday
  Writing Purpose: to narrate
  Brainstorming List: Maria and husband list all the chores
        each chooses some chores to do
        Maria dusts, straightens up
        husband vacuums, does repairs
        Maria cooks, husband sets table
        husband washes dishes, Maria dries

  Topic Sentence: _____

Lesson 2   IDENTIFYING PARAGRAPHS

A **paragraph** is made up of a topic sentence and the sentences that relate to, or **support**, the topic sentence. The topic sentence states the main idea of a paragraph. The rest of the sentences in the paragraph should relate to this main idea. If they do not, they do not form a paragraph.

Look at the following group of sentences. Do they form a paragraph?

Life insurance can be important to many families. Yesterday our company had a meeting. The life insurance agent is always very polite. I think one of my uncles sells life insurance. There are many advertisements for life insurance on television.

Although this looks like a paragraph, it is not. The topic sentence states that life insurance can be important to many families, but the remaining sentences don't explain why or how this is so. The problem is that the writer is trying to write about too many topics and has too many writing purposes. It is hard to tell what the writer's main idea is. Does the writer want to tell about a meeting, describe the agent, explain how life insurance is sold, or persuade the reader to buy it?

To decide whether a group of sentences is a paragraph, read the topic sentence. Then see if each sentence tells about the topic sentence and fits the writing purpose. In a real paragraph, such as the example that follows, the remaining sentences do relate to the topic sentence.

Life insurance can be an important part of many families' financial planning because it is helpful in a variety of situations. The primary purpose of life insurance is to provide income to the family if the wage earner dies. Life insurance can also be used as a loan to the family when it needs emergency funds. After a person retires, life insurance can supplement pension and Social Security payments.

In this example, the writing purpose and topic are clear. The topic sentence alerts the reader to look for an explanation of why life insurance can be important to families. The remaining sentences state different ways families can use life insurance. They all relate to the topic sentence.

A paragraph may contain few or many sentences. Writers must decide if they have included enough sentences to support the topic and fulfill their writing purpose.

PRACTICE

As you read each group of the following sentences, decide whether they form a paragraph. Do this by seeing if each sentence supports the topic sentence, which is shown in boldface. Write **P** in the blank space if the sentence forms a paragraph. Write **N** if they do not. The first example has been done for you.

1. _____ **Lawyers are busy people.** They handle many cases every day. On television and in movies, lawyers dress very nicely. They also lead exciting lives. Downtown, the Legal Aid office is always filled with people. When my previous landlord refused to refund my security deposit, I went to the legal aid office for advice.

2. _____ **Even though you are a law-abiding citizen, you may find yourself in situations in which you need a lawyer.** You may want a lawyer when you have been seriously injured or when the property has been seriously damaged. If you are getting a divorce and you have children, you may have to hire a lawyer. You might need a lawyer if someone sues you for a large amount of money.

3. _____ **Carlos enjoys watching television.** In the morning, he watches the morning news and weather. When he comes home from work, he watches the game shows and the evening shows. At night, he likes to watch comedies and reruns of detective shows.

4. _____ **Television plays an important role in our lives.** Carlos watches five hours of television every day. Many Americans own a color television. Children like to watch cartoons on Saturday morning. Televisions cost less than they did twenty years ago.

5. _____ **Yesterday the learning center presented GED awards.** Gina listens to the radio when she studies. A high school diploma helps you get ahead in life. I won an award once for knowing how to tie knots. The learning center opened five years ago.

6. _____ **Jose won an award for getting his equivalency diploma.** All his friends came to see him receive it. The award was presented by his teacher. Grateful for the support of his family, Jose thanked them one by one in his acceptance speech.

REVIEW EXERCISES

A. The topic sentence is missing from each of the following groups of sentences. Read the sentences and answer the questions about the topic and writing purpose. Then write the topic sentence. Remember, there is more than one way to write the topic sentence. Finally, reread the paragraph to make sure the topic sentence expresses the main idea. The first example has been done for you.

1. **Topic Sentence:** *Everyone should eat vegetables.*

   Vegetables provide people with important vitamins and minerals. Eating lots of vegetables can keep a person healthy. Whether vegetables are eaten raw or cooked, they are a tasty, nutritious, and necessary part of a balanced diet.

   What is the topic?
   Why it is important to eat vegetables.
   What is the writing purpose?
   To persuade.

2. **Topic Sentence:** _____

   My brother rescued a child from a burning building. My mother gave first aid to someone at her job who choked on food. My five-year-old cousin dialed the emergency ambulance number when her grandmother stopped breathing.

   What is the topic?
   What is the writing purpose?

3. **Topic Sentence:** _____

   A good head of lettuce has no brown spots or wilted leaves. The leaves are crisp and firm, not soggy and limp. A good head of lettuce has no bugs or clumps of dirt in it.

   What is the topic?
   What is the writing purpose?

4. **Topic Sentence:** _____

   First, the children ran out to play on the swings. Next, they looked for colorful leaves and pine cones. Later, they fed the ducks on the pond. After they fed the ducks, they sat down and ate their picnic lunches.

   What is the topic?
   What is the writing purpose?

5. **Topic Sentence:** _____

   Gardening gets you outside in the fresh air and sunshine.

Growing your own vegetables gives you a sense of accomplishment. Vegetable gardening can be a relaxing and productive hobby. The vegetables that you have planted, cared for, and harvested always seem to taste fresher than the vegetables you buy at the grocery store.

What is the topic?
What is the writing purpose?

6. Topic Sentence: _____

Empty parking lots give you a place to practice driving without having to worry about traffic. After you feel comfortable in the parking lot, drive on a quiet street. Avoid heavily traveled roads. They can be difficult for a new driver until he or she knows the traffic rules and feels comfortable behind the wheel.

What is the topic?
What is the writing purpose?

B. Each of the following items gives you the topic and writing purpose. Brainstorm three to five ideas on each topic. Then write a topic sentence for each item. The first example has been done for you.

1.   **Topic:** what you can find in a library
    Writing Purpose: to describe
    Brainstorming List: books on cooking and sewing
                           magazines on home repairs and car
                             maintenance
                         records and paintings
                         newspapers, children's books, maps
    Topic Sentence: *Our library has many different materials to look at, and read.*

2.   **Topic:** ways to find medical help
    Writing Purpose: to explain
    Brainstorming List:
    Topic Sentence: _____

3.   **Topic:** the day I interviewed for a job
    Writing Purpose: to narrate

Brainstorming List:

Topic Sentence: _____

4.   **Topic:** the different kinds of music liked by parents and by children

      Writing Purpose: to describe

      Brainstorming List:

      Topic Sentence: _____

5.   **Topic:** why handguns should (should not) be outlawed

      Writing Purpose: to persuade

      Brainstorming List:

      Topic Sentence: _____

6.   **Topic:** why I want more education

      Writing Purpose: to explain

      Brainstorming List:

      Topic Sentence: _____

Student Assignment

Write a topic sentence for your own writing or choose a topic sentence you wrote in Review Exercise B.

Prewriting Checklist

Discuss your topic sentence with your teacher or another person. Use this checklist as a guide.

1. Does my topic sentence tell who or what my paragraph will be about?
2. Does my topic sentence state my writing purpose?
3. Do I think my topic sentence will get the reader's attention?

Video Replay

In the video, Maria and Marge work on a topic sentence together. Is it easier for you to work with another person or alone? Write about whether you prefer working with someone or by yourself.

CHAPTER 4 *PREWRITING*

Supporting the Main Idea

VIDEO FOCUS

In the video, Tommy and the other parents want their children's school bus stop changed to a safer location. They have already written the topic sentence of their petition to the bus company owner. A petition is a businesslike, written request to someone in authority about a serious subject. Then they review their brainstorming list for details and examples to support the topic sentence.

Supporting their topic sentence with **details** and **examples** will give their reader a full understanding of their main idea. Details and examples can be used for any writing purpose. The details used by the group on the video consist of **facts** and **reasons**. The writers support their main idea further with examples from their own experience. In this chapter you will learn how to use facts, reasons, and examples to support your ideas. All three types of support help writers to persuade their readers.

Chapter Objectives

After seeing the video and completing the chapter, you will understand how to

- identify details (facts and reasons) that support your main idea
- use examples from your personal experience to support your main idea.

35

Key Words

Here are some important words that appear in this chapter or on the video. Notice how they are used. If a new word occurs that you do not understand, write it down and ask your teacher to explain it to you.

support   facts
supporting sentence   reasons
details   examples

Lesson 1 USING DETAILS TO SUPPORT THE TOPIC SENTENCE

In the video, the parents **support** their request for a new bus stop by describing the dangers of the present bus stop. These are **details**. The details provide specific information that helps the company owner understand the parents' concern. The information gives the owner reasons to make the requested change.

Details are particular pieces of information that help the reader understand your main idea and purpose. Details may include **facts** and **reasons**. Facts are usually details that are true or that can be proven. Reasons are logical explanations that make sense to the writer and the reader.

A topic sentence should be supported, or backed up, by ideas that fully and clearly communicate the writer's thoughts to the reader. As you think about the ideas to include in your writing, be sure that each idea or sentence relates to the topic sentence. Remember, the topic sentence expresses the main idea and the writing purpose of the paragraph. By using details to support your topic sentence, you help the reader understand, believe in, or agree with your message.

In the following paragraph, the topic sentence (shown in boldface italics) is supported by details that are facts (numbered). Each **supporting sentence** states a fact about the discussion of the ordinance at the City Council meeting, the main idea of the topic sentence.

> ***The proposed city ordinance was discussed at the City Council meeting***. **1.** Several people spoke in favor of the proposed ordinance because the law would protect everyone's rights. **2.** Others argued against the proposal because it would violate their personal freedom. **3.** The City Council decided not to vote on the proposed ordinance until more public hearings were held.

In the following paragraph, the topic sentence (shown in boldface) is supported by reasons (numbered). Each supporting sentence states a reason that explains why the writer supports the no-smoking ordinance, the main idea of the topic sentence.

> **I support the city ordinance that prohibits people from smoking in public places. 1.** Many people are allergic to smoke. **2.** Also, many nonsmokers are offended by the smell of smoke that stays on their skin and clothes. **3.** Nonsmokers have the right to breathe clean air.

PRACTICE

The following paragraphs contain a topic sentence (shown in boldface) and supporting sentences. Identify the type of support used (facts or reasons). Then add to the paragraph one or two sentences of the same type of support. Be sure that the new sentences support the topic sentence. The first exercise has been done for you.

1. **Considerate roommates are neat and clean.** They dust and vacuum the apartment regularly. They put dirty clothes and towels in the hamper, not on the bathroom floor.

Type of Support: facts
More Support: 1. Every morning, they make their bed before they leave for work.
2. After dinner, they wash the dirty dishes and put them away.

2. **I would like to train to be a computer repair person for several reasons.** Repair people are in demand because most businesses depend on computers. I like solving problems and fixing machines, so I will enjoy this job.

Type of Support:
More Support: 1.
2.

(Write one or two more sentences stating reasons.)

3. **There are several advantages to knowing how to read a road map.** The road map can help you plan the quickest route from one place to another. The map also can show you the most scenic way to travel.

Type of Support:
    More Support: 1.
                         2.

(Write one or two more sentences stating advantages.)

4. **Smoking causes many health problems for people.** Heavy smoking causes shortness of breath and fatigue. It also increases the chances of developing heart disease.

Type of Support:
    More Support: 1.
                         2.

(Write one or two more sentences stating health problems.)

Lesson 2   USING EXAMPLES TO SUPPORT THE TOPIC SENTENCE

Examples are specific statements from personal experience that illustrate a general idea.

    General Idea: Dogs bark.
        Example: My dog barked at the mailman.

You can use examples to help the reader see a picture of what you are writing about. In the following paragraph, the writer develops one example through several supporting sentences. Notice that this one example illustrates the general idea stated in the topic sentence (shown in boldface).

    Most people who smoke do not realize the damage cigarettes do to their bodies. 1. My friend smoked four packs of cigarettes a day since he was thirteen. **2.** He frequently claimed that he never had any problems with his lungs. **3.** He didn't realize that his coughing, shortness of breath, and hoarseness were related to smoking. **4.** By the time he was forty, he had lung cancer. **5.** He died before he turned forty-two.

In the following paragraph the writer uses personal examples (numbered) to support the topic sentence (shown in boldface).

> **Many people become experts at whatever they try by applying the saying, "Practice makes perfect."** **1.** My husband, who plays piano, practices for an hour every day so he can perform with a band on weekends. **2.** Our doctor, whose patients have had arthritis, cancer, and several kinds of flu, is always studying the most up-to-date treatments. **3.** My son built many tables, each one better looking than the ones he made before.

While there is no "correct" or "right" number of details or examples to include in a paragraph, most writers like to support the topic sentence with at least three statements. Your writing needs to have enough support for your audience to understand the topic and writing purpose.

PRACTICE

The following paragraphs contain a topic sentence (shown in boldface) and supporting sentences. Identify the type of support used (a single example or a variety of examples). Then add to the paragraph by writing one or two more sentences of the same type of support. When you have finished, reread the paragraph to make sure that the new sentences support the topic sentence. The first paragraph has been done for you.

1. **Some people don't know that electrical outlets should never be overloaded.** My sister didn't realize that she shouldn't plug major appliances, such as refrigerators and stoves, into the same outlet. Every time she turned on the oven part of the stove, the refrigerator stopped running. One day she plugged her vacuum cleaner into the same outlet as the dishwasher and all the lights blew.

Type of Support: single example
More Support: 1. She also ran the air conditioner and the iron from the same outlet and caused a short.
2. When she plugged the blender into the same outlet as the television, horizontal lines appeared on the screen.

2. **Workdays can be hectic.** Last week I overslept, was late to work, and missed an important meeting. Sometimes my boss needs a job done more quickly than usual. When some of our workforce does not show up, the rest of us have to work faster and longer to meet deadlines.

   Type of Support:
     More Support: 1.
                       2.

(Write one or two sentences stating causes for stress at work.)

3. **Before washing new clothes, it is important to read the clothing care label carefully.** Once I carelessly tossed a new blouse into hot water in my washing machine. When the spin cycle was over, I took out my blouse. The blouse was a bundle of uneven material.

   Type of Support:
     More Support: 1.
                       2.

(Write one or two sentences stating problems with the blouse.)

REVIEW EXERCISES

A. Decide which of the following statements are *facts*, which are *reasons*, and which are *examples*. In the blank space beside each statement, put an **F** if it is a fact, an **R** if it is a reason, and an **E** if it is a personal example. The first sentence has been done for you.

  F   1. Sleep is essential to good health.
_____ 2. Popular music is one of the big businesses in this country.
_____ 3. Because of poor inspection, the trains had many accidents.
_____ 4. On a bus or train I always sit next to the window and look out.
_____ 5. In the United States, a president is elected every four years.
_____ 6. He is not a big movie star any more because he is much older now.
_____ 7. Video games are very popular with teenagers.

_____ 8. My girlfriend and I watched a video on my VCR.

_____ 9. If you do not know basic math, you may have trouble at work.

_____ 10. My best experience at work was teaching the new man to run the computer.

_____ 11. My father likes to do woodwork in his shop on weekends.

B. For each of the following topics, write a statement you know to be true or that can be proven (*a fact*). Then write a statement about the same topic that explains something about it (*a reason*). Finally, write a statement showing how the idea actually works out (*an example*). The first topic has been done for you.

1.   **Topic:**   sleep
      Fact: *Babies need a lot of sleep when they are very young.*
      Reason: *Many people lose sleep because worries keep them awake at night.*
      Example: *When I get off my double shift, all I want to do is sleep.*

2.   **Topic:**   electing local leaders
      Fact: _____
      Reason: _____
      Example: _____

3.   **Topic:**   drugs and crime
      Fact: _____
      Reason: _____
      Example: _____

4.   **Topic:**   taxes
      Fact: _____
      Reason: _____
      Example: _____

5. **Topic:** job training

Fact: _____

Reason: _____

Example: _____

6. **Topic:** new machines in the workplace

Fact: _____

Reason: _____

Example: _____

7. **Topic:** automobile safety

Fact: _____

Reason: _____

Example: _____

8. **Topic:** diet

Fact: _____

Reason: _____

Example: _____

9. **Topic:** money

Fact: _____

Reason: _____

Example: _____

10. **Topic:** television

Fact: _____

Reason: _____

Example: _____

Student Assignment

Review the brainstorming list of ideas you wrote in Chapter 2. Decide which ideas are details or personal examples that support the topic sentence. Add any other details or personal examples you can think of to you brainstorming list. If you have no brainstorming list, add to the supporting statements you made for one of the topics in Review Exercise B.

Topic: _____

Fact 1: _____ **2:** _____

Reason 1: _____ **2:** _____

Example 1: _____ **2:** _____

Prewriting Checklist

After you have worked with your brainstorming list, discuss it with your teacher or another person. Use the checklist as a guide.

1. Did I list details (facts or reasons) that support the topic sentence?
2. Did I list my personal examples that support the topic sentence?
3. Do I have enough support for my main idea and writing purpose?

Video Replay

In the video, the parents come up with reasons for changing the school bus stop. Think of a change you would like to ask someone to make. Use facts, reasons, or personal examples to convince that person.

ON YOUR OWN

Eliminating Distracting Information

VIDEO FOCUS

In the video, Tommy and Jerry review their brainstorming list for ideas that don't relate to their topic sentence, writing purpose, and audience. Remember, they want to persuade the bus company owner to change the children's bus stop to a safer location. They eliminate the mention of the video arcade from their list because they think the bus company owner will be able to reject it. He will say that it is the parents' duty, not his, to keep the children from going into the arcade on the other side of the highway.

They also eliminate from their brainstorming list the idea, *owner should ride—see for himself.* Can you guess why they thought this idea would not relate well to the topic of safety, or help persuade the owner to change the bus stop?

Eliminating ideas that do not relate to your topic is like cleaning up a place where you are going to work. You put aside all the things that you cannot use so that you can get your hands on what you need for the job.

Chapter Objectives

After seeing the video and completing the chapter, you will understand how to

- identify information on your brainstorming list that relates to the topic sentence
- discard information on your brainstorming list that does not relate to the topic sentence.

Key Words

Here is an important phrase that appears in this chapter and on the video. Notice how it is used. If other words occur that you don't understand, write them down and ask your teacher to explain them to you.

distracting information

Lesson 1 IDENTIFYING AND ELIMINATING DISTRACTING INFORMATION

When the parents brainstormed about convincing the bus company owner to change the bus stop location, they listed every idea that people contributed. They did not stop to decide whether each idea fit the topic. Next, they went on to create the topic sentence and to identify details and examples to support it. Now, however, they must think about the value of each idea on the brainstorming list and eliminate any ideas that are distracting.

Distracting information consists of ideas that do not relate to the topic sentence, writing purpose, or audience. Such unrelated ideas are not necessary to your paragraph. A paragraph containing distracting information confuses your audience. A distracting idea will certainly weaken your writing.

You can identify distracting information by asking the following three questions about each idea on your brainstorming list:

1. Does the idea *relate* to my writing purpose?

2. Is the idea *appropriate* for my audience?

3. Does the idea *support* the topic sentence?

Look at the following list of ideas brainstormed on the specific topic, what I like about my job. The writer is already an employee. The writing purpose is to explain. The audience is a job applicant. The employer has asked his employee to write to the applicant.

good, regular hours
decent pay with overtime wages on weekends
after work, watch TV
do not work nights
friendly coworkers
fair boss
I put together computer parts
gets me out of a difficult situation at home

Topic Sentence: *There are many things that I like about my job.*

After work, watch TV is distracting information. It tells what the writer likes to do when he or she is not at work. Because this idea does not support the topic sentence, it should be crossed off the brainstorming list.

One idea on the list, *I put together computer parts*, may be true. Even if it is something the writer likes about the job, the way this idea is stated describes the job rather than explains what the writer likes about it. This distracting information does not relate to the writing purpose. Therefore, it should be crossed off the brainstorming list or changed to *I like putting together computer parts.*

Gets me out of a difficult situation at home is also distracting information. An employee's personal life has no bearing on an applicant's decision to take a similar job. This idea is not appropriate for the audience and should be crossed off the list.

Don't be surprised or upset if you find that you need to cross out several ideas from your brainstorming list. All writers come up with ideas that they eventually may want to eliminate. When you brainstormed, you were supposed to write any ideas that came to mind. Now that you are closer to writing the paragraph, you want to eliminate the ideas that will weaken your writing.

PRACTICE

For each of the following lists, read the statements of topic, writing purpose, audience, and topic sentence. First cross out the distracting information on the brainstorming list. Remember, information is distracting when it is unrelated to the topic or wrong for the writing purpose or for the audience. Then add one or more supporting ideas—facts, reasons, or examples—to the list. The ideas you add should support the topic sentence and relate to the writing purpose and audience. The first example already has been done for you.

1.
Topic:	widespread use of computers
Writing Purpose:	to explain
Audience:	your coworkers
Topic Sentence:	Everyone has contact with computers.
Brainstorming List:	microwave ovens
	digital wristwatches
	small, hand-held computers
	~~computers were invented by mathematicians~~

computerized airplane schedules
and reservations

~~repair manual shows how to fix broken~~
~~computers~~

~~some computers are the size of credit cards~~

More Support: 1. <u>computerized receipts at</u>
<u>supermarket</u>
2. <u>computers issue tickets</u>
<u>for sports events</u>

2.
Topic: the minimum wage
Writing Purpose: to persuade
Audience: your congressperson
Topic Sentence: I am opposed to lowering the
minimum wage for several
reasons.

Brainstorming List: won't reduce unemployment
workers will do less work
people will stay on welfare
some minimum wage workers
can't speak English
need more health benefits

More Support: 1. _____
2. _____

3.
Topic: my eviction notice
Writing Purpose: to persuade
Audience: city official
Topic Sentence: A city official should prevent my
landlord from evicting me.

Brainstorming List: didn't have rent money last month
landlord sent me eviction notice
not fair to treat me this way
my apartment has four rooms
parents help pay for sister's
apartment, but not mine
now I have money, but landlord
still wants me out of the building

More Support: 1. _____
2. _____

4.

Topic:	my musical cousin, Jeremy
Writing Purpose:	to describe
Audience:	record producer
Topic Sentence:	My cousin Jeremy is a musician with many talents.
Brainstorming List:	his brothers and sisters don't play music
	performs in a local band
	the club he played in last night just opened
	likes to repair cars in his spare time
	reads music
	his neighbors complain when the band practices late at night
More Support:	1. _____
	2. _____

5.

Topic:	why I should get a raise
Writing Purpose:	to persuade
Audience:	employer
Topic Sentence:	I deserve a raise for many reasons.
Brainstorming List:	I want to buy a new winter coat
	come to work on time
	my work area has three people in it
	my rent is being raised next month
	my brother is getting a raise from his employer
	my supervisor says I am ready for more responsibility
More Support:	1. _____
	2. _____

6.

Topic:	Sonia's surprise birthday party
Writing Purpose:	to narrate
Audience:	a friend of Sonia's who couldn't be at the party
Topic Sentence:	Sonia was surprised when her friends gave her a birthday party.

Brainstorming List: Dennis had the flu that week
we all shouted "Surprise!" when
   Sonia came in
Liza took pictures of Sonia
I was surprised when my spouse
   remembered our anniversary
   last month
Gerald made a large birthday
   card that everyone signed
the sofa needed recovering

More Support: 1. _____

2. _____

Student Assignment

Take out the brainstorming list you created in Chapter 2, or create one now on a topic from the following list, or a topic of your own choosing. Make sure you have identified the writing purpose and audience and have written a topic sentence. Cross out the information on your brainstorming list that does not relate to the topic, writing purpose, audience, or topic sentence. Replace the ideas you crossed out with facts, reasons, or examples that support the topic sentence.

Topics

job skills I have (would like to have)
celebrations that are special to me
the best (worst) surprise of my life
the place I would most like to visit

Topic: _____

Writing Purpose: _____

Audience: _____

Topic Sentence: _____

Brainstorming List: _____

_____

_____

More Support: _____

_____

_____

Prewriting Checklist

After you have eliminated distracting information from your brainstorming list, discuss the ideas that remain on your list with your teacher or another person. Use the checklist as a guide.

1. Does each idea relate to my writing purpose?
2. Is each idea appropriate for the audience?
3. Does each idea relate to the topic sentence?
4. Do I have enough ideas to support the topic sentence?
5. Do I need to brainstorm more ideas before I begin writing the rough draft?

Video Replay

In the video, Jerry thinks there are enough ideas on the brainstorming list. Can you think of any more ideas that Jerry might include? Write them down and share them with another person.

ON YOUR OWN

CHAPTER 6 *DRAFTING*

Writing the Rough Draft

VIDEO FOCUS

In the video, Tommy tries to start writing the petition to the bus company. He is so worried about having perfect wording, organization and spelling that he cannot complete anything or even get started. Tommy is suffering from **writer's block**—the inability to write when you want to write. He does the best thing someone with writer's block can do—he calls some friends who understand the problem. His friends help him realize that it is all right for his first draft to have a lot of mistakes. The mistakes can be fixed later.

Writing flows more easily if the writer doesn't worry about how it looks or sounds the first time around. The writing won't be either polished or perfect. That's why the first try is called the **rough draft**.

Chapter Objectives

After seeing the video and completing the chapter, you will understand how to

- free yourself from attitudes and habits that make writing difficult
- quickly get your rough draft on paper
- write a paragraph that contains a topic sentence and supporting statements.

Key Words

Here are the new, important words that appear in the chapter or on the video. Notice how they are used. If an unfamiliar word occurs that you don't understand, write it down and ask your teacher to explain it to you.

rough draft
writer's block

Lesson 1   GETTING STARTED

Jerry and Mrs. G. help Tommy get started writing his rough, or first, draft. This chapter contains several suggestions that will help you begin writing your **rough draft**.

Writing the rough draft is the end of the first stage of the writing process. You learned about the rest of this prewriting in Chapters 1–5. A rough draft is the writer's first attempt to set down on paper a group of sentences about a main idea. It isn't meant to be the final copy.

Some people feel nervous when they begin writing. If they are unable to get started, they may feel frustrated as well. This condition is called **writer's block**. It usually occurs when a person skips some or all of the prewriting steps. He or she wants the rough draft to be the one, and only, perfect copy.

The following suggestions may help you get over writer's block.

1. Write often—such as short descriptions of what happened during the day, thoughts about a particular thing or series of events, and so on.

2. Talk with another person about your problems in getting started.

3. Tell another person about your ideas.

All writers, whether they are suffering from writer's block or not, find getting started easier when they are guided by the following suggestions:

1. Find a comfortable time and place to write.

2. Give yourself time to plan your writing. This will allow you to get ready.

3. Trust that you will be able to write, even if it seems difficult at the moment.

4. Write the most interesting idea first.

5. Remember that the rough draft is like a message written in chalk on a blackboard rather than painted on a highway billboard. The first copy is not the final copy.

Lesson 2   WRITING THE ROUGH DRAFT

If you have done all the prewriting steps, you probably will not experience writer's block. You can begin to write your rough draft without fear of getting stuck. The following suggestions will help make the writing process easy and enjoyable.

1. *Try to write quickly and main a good speed.* Writing the rough draft is like riding a bicycle. The more you pedal the faster you go. If you think too much about the act of riding or if you pedal too slowly, you might fall off the bike. Likewise, if you think too much about the act of writing, or if you write too slowly, your ideas and words may stop flowing.

2. *As you write, keep your topic sentences, writing purpose, and audience in mind.* Try to get a good flow of ideas that relate to your topic sentence. If you notice that you are getting off track, refocus your attention or refer to your brainstorming list of ideas.

3. *Now is the time to concentrate on the ideas, rather than on the correctness of your writing.* Think of the rough draft as a working copy that will be improved and corrected in the later stages of the writing process. If you worry about correctness when you are writing your rough draft, you will not be able to concentrate on writing the ideas.

4. *Give yourself room to make corrections later by writing on every other line of the paper.* The lines you leave empty now can be filled with words and sentences you change or add in the next stages of the writing process.

5. *You don't have to worry about the best way to word the ideas right now.* If you cannot think of the exact word you want to use, leave a blank space and keep on writing. In the next stage, you can decide on the word that best fits the sentence.

6. *You don't have to worry about making your paper look neat right now.* Rough drafts are usually messy. Most writers use circles, lines, and other markings to show where ideas, sentences, and words are going to be rearranged. Writers also leave blank lines and spaces where they want to add ideas later. Remember that only you, not your audience, will read your rough draft.

7. *You don't have to be concerned about spelling, punctuation, and grammar right now.* If you do not know how to spell a word, write it as it sounds to you. Circle it so that later you will remember to look it up in the dictionary or ask someone the spelling. The same advice applies to punctuation and grammar. Even if you think you have made mistakes, continue writing. You can fix the mistakes later.

8. *You don't have to erase mistakes or throw away your paper because you've made a mistake.* If you notice that you have made a mistake, it's fine to cross it out or quickly correct it. Then keep on writing. Remember, creating a perfect paper is not the purpose of the rough draft.

Here is an example of a rough draft. Notice that it contains misspelled words, punctuation errors, and problems in grammar. The writer has left some sentences unfinished and has left spaces to fill in words, or one or more sentences. Some words were crossed out in one place and then used again because the person was writing fast. There is space for the writer to make more changes later on, since the rough draft is written on every other line.

The topic is *why I voted for Henry Jackson for mayor in the last election.* The purpose is to explain, because the writer is telling us why he or she voted for one candidate instead of another. The audience is the editor and readers of a newspaper where the writer will send the letter to be printed.

I voted for Henry Jackson for mayor in the last election because I ~~did not like~~ do not like the way the schools are run. ~~The schools are run~~ so that it is hard to learn in these schools. ~~Most classes I have~~ Some teachers are good, but too many classes are too big. ~~Students are~~ many classrooms are old the lights and desks are bad. When kids come late or miss school they are not disciplined enough. Henry Jackson said he would spend more and raise teacher's pay the other candidate said teachers just should be more strict and give more homework. There is not enough money, I think better pay will get better teachers to teach. Homework is important, but the good teacher can give more also.

The following is a finished, revised version of the preceding rough draft. It is an example of the kind of writing you will be able to do after you learn how to revise according to organization and style, and how to edit your work, in the following chapters.

I voted for Henry Jackson for mayor in the last election because I do not like the way the schools are run. It is hard to learn in these schools. Some teachers are good, but the classes are too big for students to get enough attention. Also, many classrooms are old. The lights in them are weak, and the desks and chairs are cracked or broken. Another problem is that students are not disciplined enough when they are late or miss school. Above all, not enough money is spent on teachers. Henry Jackson said he would spend more on new classrooms and raise teacher's pay. The other candidate just said the teachers should be more strict and give more homework. I think better pay will attract better teachers. More money also will buy more teachers, so that classes will be smaller and students will learn better. While homework and discipline are important, learning is the most important thing.

Lesson 3 MAINTAINING CONCENTRATION

When you are writing alone, you need to find a quiet, comfortable place where you can think and write as long as you may want to without being disturbed. If you find your mind beginning to wander, you may want to follow one or more of these suggestions:

1. Place a picture of your audience in front of you. Glance at it often.
2. Imagine that you are writing to an understanding friend.
3. Type your draft on a typewriter or computer.
4. Set a writing goal of a minimum number of minutes or lines.
5. Change your usual writing place. Go outside if weather permits.

PRACTICE

Use the information from one of the following topics to write a *rough draft*. For the first topic, the brainstorming list has already been done.

1.
Topic:	why the employees need a daycare center for their children
Writing Purpose:	to persuade
Audience:	the Board of Directors
Kind of Language:	formal
Brainstorming List:	no worry about special arrangements for infants can check children during breaks and at lunch if child gets sick during the day, parent nearby children are important peace of mind about childcare— we work better
Topic Sentence:	The Fairview Corporation should provide a day care center for its employees' children.
Rough Draft:	

2.   **Topic:** how my family first came to this country

    Writing Purpose: to narrate

           Audience: friends and members of your own family

  Kind of Language: everyday

      Rough Draft:

3.   **Topic:** why I want to enter a job training program

    Writing Purpose: to explain

           Audience: job application interviewer

  Kind of Language: businesslike

      Rough Draft:

4.   **Topic:** why my favorite movie star (or TV star) should be admired

    Writing Purpose: to persuade

           Audience: local contest on this topic

  Kind of Language: businesslike

      Rough Draft:

5.   **Topic:** what I like to wear when I go out (or, what I like to wear just to be comfortable)

    Writing Purpose: to describe

           Audience: friends or other students

  Kind of Language: everyday

      Rough Draft:

Student Assignment

If you have done the prewriting activities in Chapters 1–5 on a topic of your own choosing, write your rough draft now. Remember to follow the guidelines and suggestions in this chapter as you write. If you have not done the prewriting steps in Chapters 1–5, do them now. It will make writing your rough draft easier.

Drafting Checklist

After you have written your rough draft, discuss your work with your teacher or another person. If you do not have a piece of writing on a topic of your choosing, discuss the draft you wrote for the Student Assignment in this chapter. Use the checklist as a guide.

1. Did I write my rough draft at a steady speed without worrying about neatness or correctness?

2. Did I keep my topic sentence, writing purpose, and audience in mind as I wrote the rough draft?

3. If I had trouble getting started, did I try out the suggestions for getting over writer's block?

4. Did I follow the suggestions about making writing as easy and as enjoyable as possible?

5. If I got stuck after I started, did I try the suggestions for maintaining concentration?

Video Replay

In the video, Tommy has a hard time getting started because he wants his rough draft to be perfect. He doesn't realize he could fix his mistakes later. Write about a situation you or someone you know has experienced in which the wish to be perfect interfered with getting something.

UNIT 2

REVISING FOR ORGANIZATION

Now that you have written your rough draft, you are ready to move into the next stage of the writing process—revising. Revising is like rearranging the furniture in your house until you feel everything is in its right place.

Revising helps the writer improve the presentation of ideas in the rough draft. When you revise, you first review the rough draft to make sure of the following points.

1. Your purpose is clear.

2. You have adequately supported the main idea of the topic sentence.

3. You have eliminated distracting information.

Revising is a process of gradually clearing away whatever covers up the power of your ideas and the beauty of your language. It lets your writing be the best it can be.

When you revise for organization, you look carefully at the order, or sequence, of ideas in the writing. There are six main ways to organize the ideas in a paragraph. You select the way to organize your ideas according to your topic and writing purpose. Each chapter in this unit explains a different way of organizing writing.

Chapter 7: Time Order
Chapter 8: Steps in a Process
Chapter 9: Order of Importance
Chapter 10: Causes and Effects
Chapter 11: Comparison or Contrast
Chapter 12: Spatial Order

The examples and practices in each chapter help you understand each way. The chapters also show you how to decide which organization is best suited to your writing.

You probably will need to write your new rough drafts to practice some of these ways. These drafts will give you a good opportunity to review the pre-writing process. Remember to determine your purpose and audience, brainstorm, write a topic sentence, support your topic sentence, and eliminate distracting information.

ON YOUR OWN

CHAPTER 7

Time Order

VIDEO FOCUS

In the video, Robert revises a rough draft of an accident report with Tony's help. He rearranges the order of his sentences so that they tell what happened in **time order**, that is, what happened first, second, third, and so on.

Organizing ideas in correct time order helps the reader understand how something happened in time. When you write about events as they happen in time, your writing purpose is to narrate—to tell a story. You may need to do this in a letter to a friend as well as in a businesslike report such as Robert has to write. Personal letters often tell short narratives of events in a person's life.

Narrative writing can be useful and interesting for you. You may want to write a history of your family or tell the story of a happy or emotional experience in your life. If you enjoy writing regularly, you might even want to try making up stories out of your experience, using your imagination.

Chapter Objectives

After seeing the video and completing the chapter, you will understand how to

- tell if you should organize your ideas in time order
- write and revise a paragraph about a series of events as they occurred in time
- use words that make time order clearer.

Key Words

Here are some important words that appear in this chapter or on the video. Notice how they are used. If you come across a word that is not on this list, write it down and ask your teacher to explain it.

time order
signal words

Signal Words

first (second, third)	at the beginning (middle, end)
before, earlier	of the day (week, month, year)
after, later	while, meanwhile, during, when
as soon as	next, then, finally
last week (month, year)	now, today, yesterday, tomorrow

Lesson 1   ORGANIZING A SERIES OF EVENTS IN TIME ORDER

In the video, Robert revises the order of his sentences that tell about the accident so that they are in **time order**. When writers narrate a story or tell about a series of events, they arrange their sentences in time order.

To decide whether you should organize the sentences of your paragraph in time order, ask yourself the following questions about your rough draft:

1. Is my *writing purpose* to tell (narrate) a story?

2. Would my *meaning* be clearer if I wrote about the events of the story in the order in which they happened?

3. Would the sentences in the paragraph *support* the topic sentence better if they were written in *time order*?

In the following paragraph, the sentences are organized in time order. The topic is, *the errands Donna did after work*. The writing purpose is to narrate. The topic and writing purpose are expressed in the topic sentence, which is in boldface.

> **Donna had several errands to run after work.** First, she went to the bank to cash her paycheck. Then, she went to the post office to buy stamps and to mail a package. Next, she went to the grocery store to buy food for the week. Before she went home, she stopped at the hardware store to buy a new hammer and screwdriver.

The topic sentence is followed by four events, or details, that support it. Because the writer has arranged the events in the order in which they happened, the reader can easily understand which event happened first, second, third, and last.

Lesson 2 USING WORDS THAT SIGNAL TIME ORDER

Signal words help the writer move from one idea to the next in a paragraph. Different words or groups of words are used as signal words for different kinds of organization. In the following chapters you will learn about other types of signal words. Signal words also help the reader identify the way the paragraph is organized. Look for words in the paragraph about Donna's errands that signal time order.

The writer used the signal words **after, first, then, next**, and **before**. These and other words in the following list are used to signal time order. They help the reader understand the relationship of the events to each other. (Some of these words are also used in paragraphs that explain the *steps of a process*, which is another kind of organization you will learn about in the next chapter, Chapter 8.)

first (second, third)
before, earlier
after, later
as soon as
last week (month, year)
at the beginning (middle, end) of the day (week, month, year)
while, meanwhile, during, when
next, then, finally
now, today, yesterday, tomorrow

The next paragraph about Donna uses some of the signal words, to help the reader see that the ideas are organized by time order. The writer's purpose is to narrate. The topic sentence and the signal words are shown in boldface.

> **Donna came home from work and quickly did some housekeeping chores. First,** she put away the groceries. **Then,** she heated water for coffee. The water took several minutes to boil. **Meanwhile,** she noticed that the breakfast dishes were still in the sink. **While** she washed the dishes, she thought about what she would fix for dinner. **After** she finished the dishes, she sat down with her cup of coffee and recorded her bills in the family budget book.

Presenting the events in time order and using signal words that indicate time order helps the reader understand the relationship of the events to each other.

Writers also indicate time order by referring to clock time, calendar time, holidays, or usual times for certain activities.

For example, clock time tells you how to order the following two sentences.

> At nine o'clock in the morning, I sat down to write a letter.
> At ten o'clock, I made myself some coffee.

(Writing the letter happened first. Making coffee came second.)
Calendar time tells you how to order the next two sentences.

> In February, we had a blizzard.
> In March, the buds appeared on the trees.

(The blizzard came first. The buds appeared later.)

Knowing the usual time for breakfast and lunch helps you order the next two sentences.

> During breakfast, my son told me he was going to a friend's house.
> After lunch, they rode their bicycles to the swimming pool.

(The telling came first. Riding the bicycles came second.)

PRACTICE

A. The following rough draft sentences support the topic sentence, *I will never forget the day the hurricane hit our town.* However, they do not appear in correct time order. The first sentence has been numbered for you. Read the other sentences. Decide on the *time order* by asking yourself which event came second, third, and so on. Use the *signal words* and clock times to help you. Number the sentences in the correct order. When you have finished, reread the topic sentence and the supporting sentences to make sure your organization makes sense.

_____ While we were eating our evening meal, the storm hit full force.

_____ At two o'clock that afternoon, strong winds and sheets of rain forced everyone indoors for shelter.

_____ After dinner, the neighborhood lost electricity.

___1___ Huge storm clouds covered the sky around ten o'clock in the morning.

_____ Finally, the storm moved on.

_____ For most of the night, the rain and wind rattled our windows and made everyone nervous.

B. This narrative paragraph about a couple doing evening chores needs *time order signal words*. In each blank space, write a signal word that makes the time order clearer. Use signal words from the list at the beginning of the chapter. The first signal word has been inserted for you. When you have finished, reread the paragraph to make sure it makes sense.

Sarah and Josh spent the evening doing chores around the house. *Before*_____ Sarah left for the grocery store, Josh began to repair the leaking faucet. _____ Sarah returned with the groceries, Josh had finished fixing the faucet. Together, Sarah and Josh cooked dinner. _____ they listened to the evening news. _____ dinner, Josh washed the dishes _____ Sarah started the laundry. _____ Sarah and Josh relaxed by talking about their plans for the weekend.

C. This narrative paragraph is a rough draft about a company's sales during one year. The draft needs revision because the events are not organized in correct time order. The topic sentence (shown in boldface) should come first. Use the references to months and holidays to rearrange the other sentences in the correct time order. Put appropriate signal words in the two blanks (see the list of signal words at the beginning of the chapter). When you have finished, reread your revision to see if the organization makes sense.

Last year was a fantastic year in sales for our company. _____ we ran back-to-school specials in September that were very popular. _____ we increased our April sales ten percent. In January, we started a sales campaign to reach new customers. At Christmas, our staff received big and well-deserved bonuses.

A. In the previous *Practices*, you rearranged ideas into correct *time order* and added some *signal words*. In the following paragraph about the history of football, the sentences are not in correct time order. Use the references to time in the sentences to rearrange them in correct time order. When you have finished, reread the paragraph to make sure your organization makes sense. The topic sentence is in boldface.

> **Football, like many other sports, has changed a lot over the years.** In 1823, an English player grew so frustrated by his mistakes that he carried the ball, and after a while carrying became part of the game. From around the year 1200 until about 1820, football was only a kicking game. The earliest form of football probably was invented about 1150. The first college game was played between Rutgers and Princeton in New Jersey on November 6, 1869. Today, these two teams still compete in regular games.

B. In the following review exercise, the writer tells the story of how he or she lost a wallet. The sentences of the narrative, however, are not in correct time order. Rearrange the sentences according to what you think is the logical order for the series of events. Use some appropriate signal words from the list at the beginning of the chapter. You only need to use a signal word when you think it will make the writing clearer or smoother. The topic sentence is in boldface. After you revise the paragraph, reread it to see if your changes make sense.

> **Once I lost my wallet on the subway.** ＿＿＿＿＿＿ I got on the train and immediately discovered that I did not have it. ＿＿＿＿＿＿ the train came while I was looking for an address in some papers in my wallet, and I left it on a bench. ＿＿＿＿＿＿ I got off the train at the next stop and caught a train back to the station where I had left it. ＿＿＿＿＿＿ a lady phoned to tell me she had found it on the bench and would bring it to me. ＿＿＿＿＿＿ I found the wallet was not on the bench, I went to the police to report my loss.

Student Assignment

If you wrote a rough draft that presents events in time order, revise your paragraph to improve its organization and use of signal words.

If you do not have a rough draft of a paragraph that uses time order, this would be a good opportunity to try writing one. Select a topic from the following list, or choose a topic of your own. Use the prewriting instructions in chapters 1–5 to help you prepare to write. Then write your rough draft and revise it so that the events are presented in the order in which they happened.

Topics for a Paragraph Using Time Order

baby born in police car on way to hospital
fire rages as hero saves child
man holds three hostages, demands to see governor
the action of a movie I saw recently
the way my food choices have changed since I was a child
the history of my labor union
the way the neighborhood population has changed in the last few
    years
the story of how I lost and found my pet
the story of how my family came to this country
the events that led to an accident
what happened at the community meeting
what I do on a typical workday
the story of my vacation
the events that led up to my marriage (or my new job)

Revising Checklist

After you have revised your paragraph, discuss your work with your teacher or another person. Use the checklist as a guide.

1. Does my topic sentence indicate that I will be narrating a story or retelling a series of events?

2. Did I rearrange the order of my sentences to make the time order clear?

3. Did I add or change any signal words to make the time order clear?

Video Replay

In the video, Robert thinks about what happened first, second, and so on during the accident. What exciting event (an accident, a crime, a wedding, winning the lottery) have you seen or been involved in? Write about the things that happened in the order in which they occurred. Share your writing with another person.

ON YOUR OWN

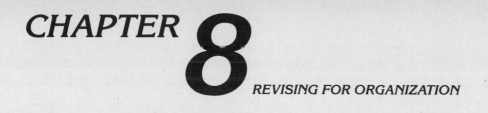

CHAPTER 8
REVISING FOR ORGANIZATION

Steps in a Process

VIDEO FOCUS

In the video, Tommy helps Terry with his paragraph on the process of changing the diaper on a baby. Jerry has included everything he needs to do but not in step-by-step order. With Tommy's help, he revises his writing.

A *process* is a series of actions or operations that produces a result, or several results. You organize your writing according to **steps in a process** when your purpose is to explain how something works, how to do something. Organizing ideas in step-by-step order is essential when you are teaching someone to do something that they do not know how to do. Only by this kind of organization will your audience understand your instructions and be able to put them into practice with the right results.

Chapter Objectives

After seeing the video and completing the chapter, you will understand how to

- tell if you should organize your ideas according to steps in a process
- write and revise a paragraph about how to do something, step-by-step
- use words that make the order of steps in a process clear.

Here are some important words that appear in this chapter or on the video. Notice how they are used. If you come across a word that does not appear on this list, write it down and ask your teacher to explain it to you.

steps in a process

Signal Words

first (second, third)	next, then, immediately
before, earlier	at this point, now
after, later	while
as soon as	finally, lastly

Lesson 1 WRITING ABOUT THE STEPS IN A PROCESS

In the video, Jerry revises his list of steps for the process of changing a diaper so that the steps are shown in correct order. When writers explain how to do something, they arrange the details so that the reader can follow the directions or instructions one step at a time. These are the **steps in a process.**

To decide whether you are writing about steps in a process, ask yourself the following questions about your rough draft:

1. Is my *writing purpose* to explain to someone how to do something?

2. Would my *meaning* be clearer if I wrote the steps in the process in the order in which they are to be done?

3. Would the sentences in the paragraph *support* the topic sentence better if they showed how to do something step by step?

Here is an example of a paragraph that shows steps in a process. The topic is *how to make a tablecloth*. The process is making a tablecloth. The writing purpose is to explain. The topic and writing purpose are expressed in the topic sentence, which is shown in boldface.

> **Making a tablecloth is easy if you follow these steps.** First, measure the size and shape of the table. Then, add 12 inches to all the measurements in order to cover the sides of the table. Next, buy the material. Now, cut the material to the exact size you want. After the material has been cut, hem the edges. Finally, iron the tablecloth.

The topic sentence is followed by six steps for making a tablecloth. These are the supporting sentences. Because the writer has arranged the steps in the order in which they should be performed, the reader can easily follow the steps. The tablecloth should fit the table perfectly.

Lesson 2   USING WORDS THAT SIGNAL STEPS IN A PROCESS

Signal words, as you learned in Chapter 7, help the writer move from one idea to the next in a paragraph. They also help the reader to identify the way the paragraph is organized. Look for words or groups of words in the paragraph about making a tablecloth that signal steps in a process.

The writer used the signal words **first, then, next, now, after**, and **finally**. These words and other words on the list at the beginning of this chapter are used to help the reader see that the organization is according to steps in a process. (Some of these words are also used in time order paragraphs, as you saw in Chapter 7.) When readers understand clearly how one step connects with the next one, they can follow directions on how to carry out a process of doing something.

The next paragraph of instructions uses some of these signal words. The topic sentence the signal words are shown in boldface italics.

> **Almost anyone can unplug a clogged sink drain.**
> **First**, remove the basket strainer from the drain. **Second**, run hot water until it stands two inches deep in the sink. **Next**, take a suction-cup plunger and place the rubber head of the plunger directly over the drain. **Then,** pump up and down quickly and forcefully until you hear the clog loosen. **After** the drain is opened, run hot water through the pipe to wash away the dirt. **Finally**, replace the basket strainer.

Presenting the steps of a process in correct order and using signal words that point up that order help the reader follow your written instructions.

PRACTICE

A. The following sentences support the topic sentence, *Making an omelet is easy if you follow these steps.* However, the supporting sentences do not appear in the correct order. Read the sentences. Decide on the correct order by asking yourself which step has to be done first, second, and so on. Use the signal words to help you decide the correct order. Number the sentences in the correct order. The first sentence has been numbered for you. When you have finished, reread the topic sentence and the supporting sentences to make sure your order makes sense.

_____ When the butter starts to sizzle, pour the eggs gently into the skillet.

_____ As soon as the cheese melts, lower the heat and use a spatula to fold the omelet in half.

_1_ First, crack two eggs into a bowl and scramble them with a fork.

_____ While you are preparing the filling, heat the skillet on medium high and add a pat of butter to grease the pan.

_____ Next, make the filling by dicing two green onions, chopping some ham, and grating the cheese.

_____ Carefully lift the omelet out of the skillet onto a plate and serve immediately.

_____ When the eggs are almost cooked, spread the filling evenly over the eggs.

B. This paragraph needs signal words to help the reader follow *steps in the process* of making pizza. In each blank space, write a signal word that makes the order of the steps clear. Use some of the signal words listed at the beginning of this chapter. The first signal word has been inserted for you. When you have finished, reread the paragraph to make sure your organization makes sense.

You can make a pizza in seven easy steps.
_____ make the dough for the crust. _____ you make the dough, preheat the oven to 350 degrees. _____ spread the tomato herb sauce over the dough. _____ chop the toppings, such as onions, green peppers, or mushrooms. _____ you place the toppings on the pizza, sprinkle grated cheese over the toppings. _____ bake the pizza for 35 minutes. _____ take the pizza out of the oven, cut it into slices, and serve immediately.

C. This paragraph lists *steps in the process* of finding a book in the library, but the steps are not in order. Reread the paragraph. Then revise it. The topic sentence (shown in boldface) should come first. Then arrange the details in the correct order, and when you have finished, reread the paragraph to make sure your organization makes sense.

1. You can find a book in the library by a simple, six-step process when you know the author's name. 2. Notice the book's number on the card with the title of the book you want. **3.** Check the numbers on the books on the shelves until you come to the exact book you are looking for. **4.** Go to the shelves that contain books with the first three numbers of the book number. **5.** Write the author's name, the title of the book, and the book's number on a piece of paper. **6.** Find the author's name and look for the title of the book. **7.** Go to the card catalog and look up the author's last name.

Student Assignment

If you wrote a paragraph about how to do something, revise your rough draft to improve its organization and use of signal words.

If you have not written a rough draft of a paragraph explaining steps in a process, this would be a good opportunity to try writing one. Write a paragraph on one of the topics listed following or on a topic of your own choosing. Use the prewriting instructions in Chapters 1–5 to help you to prepare to write. Then write your rough draft and revise it so that the steps in the process appear in the correct order.

Topics for a Paragraph Using Steps in a Process

how to wax a car

how to change a flat tire on a car (bicycle)

how to program a VCR to record when you are not home

how to transplant a potted plant

how to plant a garden

how to paint a room

how to complete income tax forms

how to complete an application for a job

how to fix a small household appliance

how to take a baby's temperature

how to sew a dress pattern (or repair a piece of clothing)

how to adopt a child

how to fix a leaky faucet

how to find a doctor in the Yellow Pages

how to cook a favorite recipe

how to build a piece of carpentry (or weave a piece of fabric)

how to play a guitar (or other musical instrument)

Revising Checklist

After you have revised your paragraph, discuss your work with your teacher or another person. Use the checklist as a guide.

1. Does my topic sentence indicate that I will be explaining how to do something?

2. Did I rearrange the order of my sentences to make the steps in the process clear?

3. Did I add or change any signal words in order to make the steps in the process clear?

Video Replay

In the video, Jerry realizes he has skipped the step of removing the dirty diaper. Have you ever tried to do something and skipped one or more steps? Write about what happened, and share it with another person.

9

Order of Importance

VIDEO FOCUS

In the video, Jolene reorganizes a job application letter to a new employer. Since companies get many such letters, Jolene wants hers to stand out. She decides to list the things she has to offer in the order of importance, starting with what she decides will be most important to the employer. Her purpose is to persuade the employer to hire her for the job. Her letter will be most persuasive if she puts the strongest reasons why the employer should do this as her first supporting sentences.

You can influence your reader's attitudes by organizing your writing to emphasize what is most important. Ideas organized by **order of importance** capture the reader's attention right away and make a good first impression.

Chapter Objectives

After seeing the video and completing the chapter, you will understand how to

- tell if you should organize your ideas by order of importance
- sort out the more important ideas from the less important ideas
- revise a persuasive paragraph according to order of importance
- use signal words that make the order of importance clearer.

Key Words

Here are some important words that appear in this chapter or on the video. Notice how they are used. If you come across a word that does not appear on this list, write it down and ask your teacher to explain it to you.

order of importance

Signal Words

first (second, third)	another reason
most (least, less, equally) important	also
most (least, less, equally) significant	in addition
best (main, primary) reason	above all
	finally

Lesson 1 ORGANIZING REASONS IN ORDER OF IMPORTANCE

In the video, Jolene organizes her letter to a new employer according to **order of importance** because the purpose of her letter is to persuade. If she wrote her topic as a title for her letter it would be, *why you should hire me for the job of receptionist*. When writers want to persuade readers to agree with them, they often arrange their reasons in order of importance.

Organization by order of importance means that you put your most important reason right after the topic sentence. Then, you put your next-most important reason, and then the less important reasons. The least important reason comes in the last sentence. In other words, all the supporting sentences of the paragraph are put in an order from the most important, to the less important, to the least important. If you put the most important reasons in this order in the first supporting sentences, your writing should make such a strong impression that the less important reasons also will look stronger.

In the video, Jolene decides that her two strong points are, first, her fifteen years of work experience and second, her cheerful, friendly personality. The other reasons she gives—that she is taking a class in office skills and that she is always on time for work—are less important, she decides. She therefore revises her paragraph to put the two most important ideas first and second, and the other two ideas third and last.

To decide whether you should organize your ideas according to the order of importance, ask yourself the following questions about your rough draft.

1. Is my *writing purpose* to persuade my audience to my point of view?

2. Would my *meaning* be clearer if I listed reasons in the order of importance?

3. Would the sentences in the paragraph *support* the topic sentence better if they were organized in the order of importance?

Here is an example of a persuasive paragraph that lists reasons in the order of importance. The topic is, *why smoke detectors should be installed in apartments*. The writing purpose is to persuade. The topic and writing purpose are expressed in the topic sentence, which is shown in boldface.

Smoke detectors should be installed in all apartments. The most important reason is that smoke detectors save hundreds of lives and much property every year by warning people of fire. A second reason to install smoke detectors is that they give people living in apartment buildings a sense of security. Third, these machines should be installed because they offer this protection for a small price. Finally, the detectors need very little maintenance.

The topic sentence is followed by four reasons that support it. Notice that the most important reason—smoke detectors save lives and property—is placed immediately after the topic sentence. The next reason—smoke detectors offer a sense of security—is less important than the first reason. The other reasons—low price and little maintenance—are less important, and therefore are put in the third and fourth sentences. Because the writer has arranged the ideas in order of importance (from the most important to the least important), the reader knows exactly where to focus his or her attention.

Lesson 2   USING WORDS THAT SIGNAL THE ORDER OF IMPORTANCE

Signal words, as you have learned in the previous chapters, help the writer move from one idea to the next in a paragraph. They also help the reader identify the way the paragraph is organized. Look for the words or groups of words in the paragraph about smoke detectors that signal order of importance.

The writer used the signal words **most important reason, a second reason**, and **third**. These and other words in the list at the beginning are used to show the order of importance. They point out the relative importance of each reason.

The next persuasive paragraph uses some of these signal words. The topic is, electing Marcus as our representative. The topic sentence and the signal words are shown in boldface.

We should elect Marcus to be our labor representative. First, he has worked with us for eight years, so he understands our concerns. **Second,** we can trust him because he is loyal. **Also**, he is dependable and will always do what we need when we need it. **In addition**, he is assertive and will work as an equal with a management team. **Finally**, Marcus is a good public speaker.

By arranging the reasons in order of their importance and using signal words effectively, you help the reader understand your ideas.

PRACTICE

A. These sentences support the topic sentence, *Our neighborhood needs a school bus stop on our block at the corner of Central Avenue and Third Street*. However, the reasons do not appear in most-to-least order of importance. Read the sentences. Decide on the correct order by asking yourself which reason is most important, less important, and least important. Use the signal words to help you decide on the correct order. Then, number the sentences so that the reasons are listed from most important to least important. The first sentence has been numbered for you. When you have finished, reread the topic sentence and the supporting sentences to make sure your organization makes sense.

_____ Also, several families with a lot of children live near the corner of Central Avenue and Third Street, and they could watch all their kids get on the bus together.

_____ Another reason is that this new bus stop would be a shorter, more convenient walk for the ten children who live near our corner.

_1_ Above all, it is unsafe for our children to cross four busy streets to get to the present bus stop.

_____ A second reason is that it is not healthy for children to walk the four blocks home from the present bus stop in extremely cold weather.

B. This persuasive paragraph needs signal words to help the reader understand the relative importance of reasons for wearing seat belts. In each blank space, write a word that makes the order of importance clear. Use some of the signal words listed at the beginning of the chapter. The first signal word has been inserted for you. When you have finished, reread the paragraph to make sure your organization makes sense.

Wearing seat belts is important for many reasons. The most significant reason is that seat belts prevent you from being thrown out of the car and killed during an accident. _____ seat belts can protect you from minor injuries such as a broken arm or a bruised forehead when the car stops suddenly. _____ seat belts are easy to use the take only a few seconds to snap into place. _____ the new seat belts are comfortable to wear and do not restrict your normal movement in the car.

C. This paragraph list reasons why the writer wants a refund on a shirt he or she has bought. The paragraph, however, does not list the reasons in order of importance. Read the paragraph. Then revise it. The topic sentence (shown in boldface) should come first. It should be followed by the reasons, listed in order from the most important to the least important. Use the signal words to organize the paragraph. When you have finished, reread the paragraph to make sure your organization makes sense.

1. I am writing to ask for a refund on the shirt that I purchased from your catalog. 2. Another reason is that your medium shirt size is not the standard medium size, so the sleeves are a little long. **3.** Finally, the color of the shirt is not exactly the same as the color pictured in your catalog. **4.** The primary reason is that the material of the right sleeve has a hole in it.

REVIEW EXERCISES

A. The topic of the following paragraph is why driver education should be required. Write a topic sentence for the paragraph. The sentences are not listed in order of importance. Revise the paragraph to put them in what you think is the correct order. No blanks have been placed in the paragraph for signal words, but you should use one or two to help connect the sentences and make the writing smoother.

_____

(topic sentence)

A number of people have not had driver education will fail the driving test and have to take it over again. Some drivers who learn on their own are dangerous because they were not taught in a school to respect the driving laws. Home-trained drivers may learn from parents or relatives who are impatient with them.

B. The topic of the following paragraph is, *why I am in favor of lotteries*. Write a topic sentence for the paragraph. The sentences are not organized in order of importance from most important, to less important, to least important. Revise to put them in what you think is the best order. There is no one correct order for these sentences. Put them in the order you think will be the most persuasive. Use some signal words to make the writing flow more smoothly.

(topic sentence)

Every time you buy your ticket, you can dream of winning and feel high for a little while. Sometimes a person wins a huge prize and has no more money worries for the rest of his or her life. If you don't spend your extra money on a lottery ticket, you are likely to spend it on some other kind of entertainment. You can win small amounts that pay for the tickets you buy.

Student Assignment

If you wrote your rough draft with the purpose to persuade, revise it to improve its organization, and use some signal words. If you do not have a rough draft of a persuasive paragraph, this would be a good opportunity to try writing one. Select a topic from the following list or choose a topic of your own. Use the prewriting instructions in Chapters 1–5 to help you prepare to write. Then write your rough draft and revise it so that the reasons appear in order of importance from most important to least important.

Topics for a Persuasive Paragraph

why I should get a raise
why a microwave oven is needed in the employees' lunch room
why parents should attend open house at their children's school
why people should not buy lottery tickets.
why new parents should attend parenting classes
why people should vote in local elections
why tenants should form a tenants' organization
why young children should not be left alone at home
why a new city bus route is needed
why people should follow their dreams

Revising Checklist

After you have revised your paragraph, discuss your work with your teacher or another person. Use the checklist as a guide.

1. Did I need to list my reasons in order of importance to fit my writing purpose?

2. Does my topic sentence indicate that I will be persuading my audience to agree with my ideas?

3. Did I rearrange the order of my reasons to make their order of importance clear?

4. Did I add or change any signal words to make the order of importance clearer?

Video Replay

In the video, Jolene decides that her work experience is the most important quality she can offer an employer. If you were looking for a job, what quality or skill would you list first? Write about your abilities and share your writing with another person.

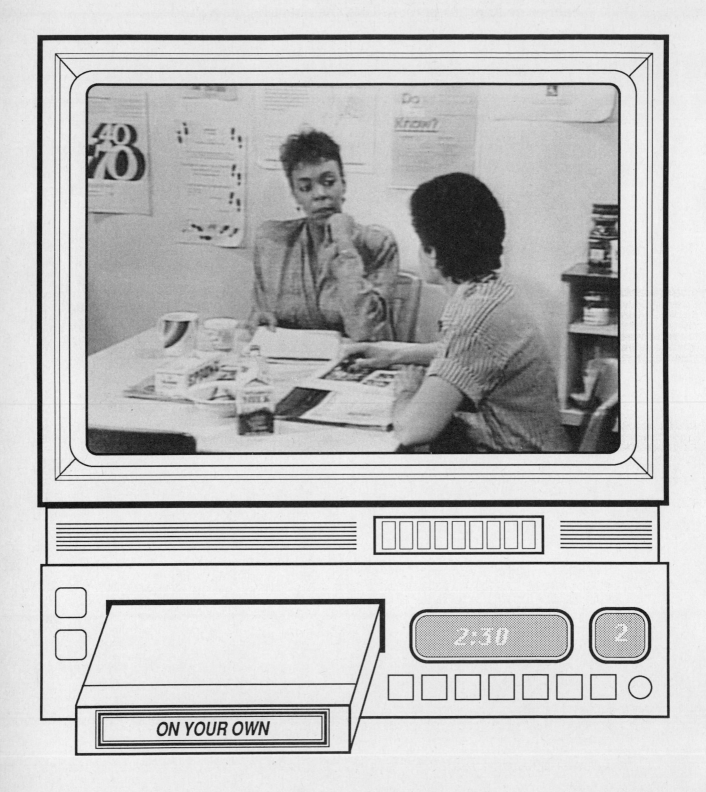

ON YOUR OWN

10

Causes and Effects

VIDEO FOCUS

In the video, Sharon writes to the city records office for a copy of her birth certificate. A new law states that after January 1, 1988, everyone must prove U.S. citizenship in order to be hired for a job. In her letter, Sharon explains that she must have her birth records in order to get employment.

Sharon's letter is organized according to **causes** and **effects**. When a writer explains something, he or she writes about causes, which are what makes something happen, and effects, which are the things that happen.

Often in your writing, your purpose will be to explain, as in a business letter, or in an essay on a topic you may have to explain why you also believe one thing instead of another. Many topics like this are on the GED Writing Sample Test. Knowing how to organize your ideas according to causes and effects is therefore one of the most important kinds of organization that you can learn.

This kind of organization includes two basic types—**effect-and-causes**, and **cause-and-effects**. Sharon uses effect-and-causes. You will study and practice both types in this chapter.

Chapter Objectives

After seeing the video and completing this chapter, you will understand how to

- distinguish between causes and effects
- tell if you should organize your thoughts according to a cause-and-effect pattern
- write and revise an effect-and-causes paragraph
- write and revise a cause-and-effects paragraph

Key Words

Here are some important words that appear in this chapter or on the video. Notice how they are used. If you come across a word that does not appear on this list, write it down and ask your teacher to explain it to you.

cause
effect

Signal Words

because	so
because of	then
if	as a result
since	as a result of
for	therefore
so that	thus
	consequently

Lesson 1   WRITING ABOUT CAUSES AND EFFECTS

A **cause** is what makes something happen. The thing that happens is called the **effect**. Sometimes we talk and write about the cause first, and other times about the effect first. In the following sentences about causes and effects, sometimes the effect appears first, and sometimes the cause is first.

> Because he is a heavy smoker (*cause*), my father had a heart attack (*effect*).

> No-brand products are cheaper than brand-name products (*effect*), since no advertising costs are added to their price (*cause*).

> Because of the pressure of production deadlines (*cause*), workers often feel stress on the job (*effect*).

> Jim is friendly but outspoken (*effect*), because his parents taught him both to respect people and to demand respect (*cause*).

These are examples of causes and effects in the same sentence. There is no one way to write about causes and effects. You may write about them either way—according to cause-and-effects or effect-and-causes. You also can write about causes and effects in a paragraph.

Write in the way that is the most comfortable for you. Look at these examples.

> Sheila was very tired. (*cause*) Therefore, she fell asleep while watching television. (*effect*) Also, she spilled her coffee. (*effect*)

> I did not see Carla all week for several reasons. (*effect*) I worked overtime three nights. (*cause*) I also was out of town for two days. (*cause*)

In the video, Sharon puts her request for a copy of her birth certificate in her topic sentence, and then gives the reasons for her request—that her new employer demands proof of her citizenship, and that she has lost her original certificate. Her request is the effect. Her reasons are the causes.

Effect	*Causes*
I need you to send me a copy of my birth certificate as soon as possible.	My new employer told me that I had to show proof of citizenship.
(topic sentence)	Every new employee is required to do this by the Immigration, Reform and Control Act.
	I cannot find my original birth certificate.
	(supporting sentences)

When you are writing about causes and effects, therefore, you can use two basic ways of organizing a paragraph:

- You can put the effect in the topic sentence, and use the supporting sentences in the paragraph to state the causes.
- You can put the cause in the topic sentence, and use the supporting sentences to state the effects.

A. The following five topic sentences state effects. For each effect, write two supporting sentences that state a cause. The first two cause sentences have been written for you.

1. **Effect:** My parents had a wonderful vacation for several
   reasons.
   Cause: *All their grandchildren visited them.*
   Cause: *My sister came to see them from Chicago.*

2. **Effect:** I would like to ask for a job-transfer for several reasons.
   Cause: _____
   Cause: _____

3. **Effect:** The family next door is moving out because of several
   things that happened.
   Cause: _____
   Cause: _____

4. **Effect:** Thomas is angry with his daughter.
   Cause: _____
   Cause: _____

5. **Effect:** Sheila got a promotion.
   Cause: _____
   Cause: _____

B. The following five topic sentences state causes. For each cause, write two supporting sentences that state an effect. The first two effect sentences have been written for you.

1. **Cause:** The fire in our apartment caused a lot of damage.
   Effect: *All our furniture was ruined.*
   Effect: *My wife's favorite dress turned black.*

2. **Cause:** I went shopping without taking enough money.
   Effect: _____
   Effect: _____

3. **Cause:** Mrs. Simpson won the lottery.
   Effect: _____
   Effect: _____

4. **Cause:** The bad weather made my bus late.
   Effect: _____
   Effect: _____

5. **Cause:** The mayor cut the school budget.
   Effect: _____
   Effect: _____

Lesson 2 WRITING AN EFFECT-AND-CAUSES PARAGRAPH

In an effect-and-cause paragraph, the topic sentence states the effect and the supporting sentences give the causes that explain the effect. Look at this paragraph written from the first topic sentence in **Practice A**.

> My parents had a wonderful vacation for several reasons. (*topic sentence stating an effect*) All their grandchildren visited them. My sister came to see them from Chicago. Then, we all went to the beach. When we got home, they celebrated their silver wedding anniversary. (*supporting sentences stating causes*)

The following chart lists a single effect *auto accidents* and a number of causes for the topic, *the causes of auto accidents*. Making a chart like this one can help you gather ideas for a paragraph that explains the causes of something, such as the following one on auto accidents.

Effect	*Causes*
auto accidents	not taking care of car
	not watching traffic
	drinking and driving
	arguing with a passenger
	driving too fast

Notice that the topic sentence states the effect that the paragraph explains.

> **There are many causes of automobile accidents.** Not taking care of a car may cause an accident, **since** defective or worn-out brakes can fail. Some accidents happen when the driver is not watching traffic. Drivers also lose control of their cars **as a result of** drinking and then driving. **Because of** an argument with a passenger, a driver may get upset and cause an accident, too. Driving too fast for road conditions is also a common cause of these disasters.

Notice that the writer uses signal words, shown in boldface. These words lead the reader from one thought to another by connecting them logically. They make the writing flow, and they emphasize that the paragraph is about causes and effects.

Sometimes a paragraph organized according to causes and effects does not use any signal words—like the preceding one on the parents' vacation. Signal words, however, may help your reader follow your explanation, and therefore you should learn how to use them.

PRACTICE

Paragraphs

A. In the following paragraph, Sharon's cold is the effect, and the supporting sentences explain the causes of her cold. Read the paragraph, and fill in the blanks with signal words.

B. In this effect-and-causes paragraph about what is making Jorge feel good, fill in the blanks with one of the signal words listed at the beginning of the chapter.

A number of things are making Jorge feel good this week. _____ he is in love now, he is happy about his life. He found out that his sick mother is better. He has learned to solve problems with his coworkers _____ he feels more secure in his job. _____ he passed the test for on-the-job training, his boss says he may get a raise, too.

Sharon has a really bad cold for several reasons. She did not get enough sleep for several nights. Her apartment had no heat for a week. _____ she caught a chill. _____ her rundown condition, she was not eating well. She could not avoid getting sick _____ her supervisor came to work with a bad cold last week, and they had to work long, hard hours.

C. Write an effect-and-causes paragraph. From the following list, use one of the topic sentences that state an effect, or make up your own effect topic sentence. Prepare yourself for writing with the prewriting steps you learned in Chapters 1–5. Then write your rough draft, and revise it so that the supporting sentences explain your topic sentence.

I would like a pay raise for several reasons.

Jamie wants a new job as a result of things that have happened in his life.

I would like to talk with my supervisor because of changes in our workplace.

The bus service (or train or subway service) is worse this year.

Joel wants a new lease for his apartment.

There is more (or less) crime on my street this year, for several reasons.

I have less (or more) money to spend this year.

I am feeling better about myself now than I did this time last year.

Lesson 3 WRITING A CAUSE-AND-EFFECTS PARAGRAPH

In a cause-and-effects paragraph, the topic sentence states the cause and the supporting sentences state the effects of the cause. The topic sentence explain these effects. Look at this cause-and-effects paragraph.

> The fire in our apartment caused a lot of damage. (*topic sentence stating a cause*) All our furniture was ruined. My wife's favorite dress turned black. Her winter coat and my best shoes were destroyed. Our immigration papers also were lost in the blaze. (*supporting sentences stating effects*)

The following chart lists a single cause (the closing of a clothing factory) and a number of effects of this cause. The topic is the effects of closing the clothing factory. Making a chart like this one can help you gather ideas for a paragraph that explains the effects of something, such as the closing of a factory.

Cause	*Effects*
the closing of the clothing factory	600 people out of work at once unemployment office opens late crafts cooperative organized to sell handmade products building receives no rent

Notice that the topic sentence states the cause. The effects are given by the supporting sentences of the paragraph.

> The closing of the clothing factory changed our town in a number of ways. Six hundred workers became unemployed at once **because of** the closing. The unemployment office had to stay open late, **since** all the workers at the factory received unemployment benefits. The unemployed workers realized how serious their situation was. **As a result**, they organized a crafts cooperative to sell handmade items such as clothes,

toys, and furniture. **Because** the factory building no longer had a tenant, the owner received no rent for it, but he still had to pay property taxes.

Notice that the writer uses signal words, shown in boldface. These words lead the reader from one thought to another by connecting them logically. They make the writing flow, and help the reader follow the explanation.

PRACTICE

A. Read the following cause-and-effects paragraph about some effects television has had on family life. Then write signal words in the blank spaces.

> Television has had good and bad effects on family life. Family members are able to share experiences, as they can watch a show together. Educational TV shows can help both parents and children learn about new things. On the other hand, children may spend too much time in front of the television, and _____ they may be less active than they should be. Some parents use TV as a babysitter _____ their children are neglected and get less attention than before.

B. The following cause-and-effects paragraph about Gloria getting a job also needs signal words to make the writing flow and to emphasize the connections of cause and effect between one thought and the next. Use signal words from the list at the beginning of the chapter. When you have finished, reread the paragraph to make sure it makes sense.

> Getting a job has resulted in many changes in Gloria's life. She has learned the importance of being on time. She has had the chance to meet new people at work and make new friends. She has more self-confidence _____ they gave her new responsibilities. Her family cannot tell her what to do so much anymore _____ she feels more independent earning her own income. _____ Gloria continues to perform well, her supervisor says she will promote her and give her a raise.

C. Write a cause-and-effects paragraph. Select a topic from the following list or choose a topic of your own. Use the prewriting instructions in Chapters 1–5 to help you prepare. Then write your rough draft and revise it so that the supporting sentences explain your topic sentence.

Mark's life changed in many ways when he gave up drinking (or smoking, drugs, or overeating).

My lifestyle changed when I bought a VCR (or another appliance, or a new vehicle, or article of clothing).

Jose saves money now in a number of ways.

Carol has found several new ways to make money.

The opening of the new day care center (or learning center) has changed our lives in several ways.

Keeping a personal budget has changed my life in many ways.

Learning to write better already has helped me in my life in several ways.

REVIEW EXERCISE

1. The following paragraph is on the topic *why single working mothers with small children have difficult lives.* Read the paragraph.

    • Is this an effect-and-causes paragraph or a cause-and-effects paragraph?
    • Write a topic sentence for the paragraph, once you have decided what type of paragraph it is.
    • Use the appropriate signal words to fill in the two blanks.

    _____

    (topic sentence)

    Some people are unfriendly to them because they do not have husbands. They are alone a great deal _____ they do not have much free time to meet people and have a social life. They have to spend a lot of their pay for babysitters. Most of them can afford to have only one child _____ they do not earn a great deal of money. If there is only one child and one parent, it is sometimes difficult for both of them.

2. The following paragraph is on the topic, *why regular exercise is a good thing.* Read the paragraph and do the following exercises.

    • Is this an effect-and-causes paragraph or a cause-and-effects paragraph?

- Write a topic sentence for the paragraph, once you have decided what type of paragraph it is.
- Use appropriate signal words to fill in the two blanks.

(topic sentence)

Regular physical exercise makes your heart stronger and gives you a better chance of living a long life. Your body will feel more relaxed, and _____ you will not get tired so easily. Since you will want to have plenty of breath for exercise, you will find it easier to cut down on smoking. Energetic exercise uses up a lot of calories _____ you also will keep your weight down.

Student Assignment

Revise each rough draft to improve its organization and use of signal words.

Revising Checklist

After you have revised each paragraph, discuss your work with your teacher or another person. Use the checklist as a guide.

1. Is my paragraph organized clearly into either a cause-and-effects paragraph or an effect-and-causes paragraph? (Make a chart, such as those on pages 91 and 92 to check your organization.)

2. If you wrote a cause-and-effects paragraph, ask yourself: (a) Does my topic sentence clearly state a cause? (b) Do the supporting sentences all state effects of this cause? (c) Do all the effects follow logically from the cause?

3. If I wrote you an effect-and-causes paragraph, ask yourself: (a) Does my topic sentence clearly state an effect? (b) Do all the supporting sentences state causes for this effect? (c) Do all the causes clearly explain the effect?

4. Are my supporting sentences in the best order to make my explanation clear?

5. Have I used some signal words to connect my sentences logically and make the writing flow?

Video Replay

In the video, Sharon writes a businesslike letter to the city records office, asking for a copy of her birth certificate. Have you ever tried to get something from a local, state, or federal government agency? Write a short rough draft about your experience. Share your writing with another person.

ON YOUR OWN

Comparison or Contrast

VIDEO FOCUS

In the video, Tony shows his son Luis how he has organized his letter to a mail order company from which he ordered a metal safe for his money. In the letter, he complains that he has not received the safe that he expected to get. He points out the differences between the catalog description of the safe and the safe they sent him. Luis helps his father revise his letter to make these differences clearer.

Tony has written a paragraph of **contrast**. When you **contrast** two things, you point out the **differences** between them. On the other hand, when you point out how two things are like each other, you are writing a paragraph of **comparison**. When you **compare** two things, you point out the ways they are alike, or similar. Instead of pointing out differences, you point out **similarities**.

Chapter Objectives

After seeing the video and completing this chapter, you will understand how to

- distinguish between differences and similarities
- tell if you should organize your ideas using contrast or comparison
- write and revise a paragraph of contrast
- write and revise a paragraph of comparison
- use signal words that help make your contrast or comparison clearer.

Here are some important words that appear in this chapter or on the video. Notice how they are used. If you come across a word that does not appear on this list, write it down and ask your teacher to explain it.

compare   contrast   similar
comparison   similarity, similarities

For comparison: alike, also, both, common, equally, in the same way, just as/so, likewise, same, too, similar, similarly

For contrast: although, but, differ, different, however, in contrast, on the other hand, unlike, whereas, while

Lesson 1   WRITING COMPARISONS OR CONTRASTS

In the video, Tony's paragraph explains how two things are different. When writers show how two people, places, things, or ideas are different, they are making a **contrast**. When they describe how two people, places, things, or ideas are alike, they are making a **comparison**.

Here are some examples of contrast:

People: Jorge has always lived in Miami. **However**, Nick just moved here.

Places: The shopping mall on Route 1 has many discount stores. **On the other hand**, the shopping mall on Route 5 has mostly high-priced stores.

Things: My union dues have remained the same for the last three years, **whereas** my neighbor's union dues have risen 5 percent each year.

Ideas: Sailing from Europe to North America in the seventeenth century took several months. **In contrast**, flying in a jet airplane from Europe to New York now takes less than a day.

Here are some examples of comparison:

People: **Both** Molly and Charlie have lived in Springfield all their lives.

Places: The shopping malls on Route 1 and Route 5 are of **similar** size.

Things: The dues are the **same** for my union and my neighbor's union.

Ideas: Exploring North America in the fourteenth century led to the discovery of new plants and animals. **Likewise**, exploring outer space now may lead to the discovery of new life forms.

PRACTICE

Identify the contrasts, or the statements that point out differences, with a **D**. Identify the comparisons, or the statements that point out similarities, with an **S**. The first statement is done for you.

__S__ 1. Both my son and my daughter have blue eyes.

_____ 2. Their son has brown hair, but their daughter's hair is black.

_____ 3. Unlike reckless drivers, defensive drivers observe traffic safety rules.

_____ 4. This handmade lamp is made out of pine wood, but that handcrafted cakebox is made out of tin.

_____ 5. While Tim's car is newer, my car is more reliable.

_____ 6. Land in Florida is flat, whereas land in Iowa is hilly.

_____ 7. The two women are equally smart.

_____ 8. Jorge showed a lot of courage by coming back to school, while Sam was afraid to try again.

_____ 9. My workplace has bright lights and is noisy, whereas my home has soft lights and is quiet.

_____ 10. Tony and Randolph supervise their employees in similar ways.

_____ 11. Doing my job well makes me happy. Getting paid too little, on the other hand, makes me unhappy.

_____ 12. Virginia's red dress sparkled with silver sequins, whereas Lydia's dress was a dark shade of blue.

_____ 13. While the indoor swimming pool is open at night, the outdoor swimming pool closes at five o'clock.

_____ **14.** The first speaker said she would cut military spending if she was elected. Likewise, the other candidates promised to cut the budget.

_____ **15.** Their feelings about religion were very much alike.

_____ **16.** Exercise and a good diet are equally important.

_____ **17.** My friend is six feet tall, whereas I am only 5 feet 7 inches tall.

_____ **18.** His oldest daughter is happy in her marriage, and his oldest son also has a good family life.

_____ **19.** My parents are Catholic, although my friends and I are interested in Oriental religion.

_____ **20.** Just as the beach I vacationed at last summer had a lot of night life, so the beach I will go to next summer has many dance clubs.

Lesson 2 WRITING A PARAGRAPH OF CONTRAST

A paragraph of contrast explains how people, places, things, or ideas are different, or not alike. Here are some examples of topics for a paragraph of contrast.

People: employer and employee attitudes, male and female attitudes on any topic, interests of retired people and working people, attitudes of parents and children on any topic, my ideas about honest and dishonest people

Places: home and workplace, two different places I have worked, two different places where I would like to retire, the country my family comes from and this country

Things: fast food and home cooking, a handmade product and a manufactured product of the same thing, two different recipes for the same dish, two different computers

Ideas: fear and courage, moral strength and moral weakness, good leadership and bad leadership, self-respect and self-dislike

In a paragraph of contrast, the topic sentence states that two people, places, things, or ideas are different, and lets the reader know that an explanation of the differences will follow. For the topic, _the differences between baseball and football,_ the topic sentence is _Baseball and football are different in several ways._ The writer will contrast season of playing, number of players, size of players, and style of uniforms.

Baseball and football are different in several ways.
Baseball is played in the spring and summer, whereas
football is a fall and winter sport. While baseball teams have
nine players, football teams have eleven. Baseball players
don't have to be especially large, but size and weight are
advantages in football. Unlike baseball uniforms, which are
light summer clothing, football uniforms must be heavily
padded for protection.

In the preceding paragraph, baseball is always mentioned first.
Keeping the same order each time makes the contrasts easy to
understand.

Lesson 3   USING WORDS THAT SIGNAL CONTRAST

Look for words in the paragraph about baseball and football that signal contrast. If you found **different, whereas, while, although, but**,
and **unlike**, you are on the right track. These and other words that
signal contrast are listed at the beginning of the chapter.

The next paragraph of contrast about rivers uses some of these
signal words. The topic is *the differences between polluted and unpolluted rivers*. The purpose is to explain the topic sentence and the signal
words are shown in boldface italics.

**A polluted river and an unpolluted river differ in
several ways.** The water in a polluted river is unsafe to
drink. **In contrast**, you can drink the water from unpolluted
rivers without worrying about getting sick. Polluted rivers
often smell of garbage and chemicals. Unpolluted rivers, **on
the other hand**, smell of sun and greenery. Some people
accept polluted rivers as the price of technological progress.
However, other people think we must have a clean
environment to survive.

By using signal words, the writer helps the reader understand the
contrast between polluted and unpolluted rivers.

PRACTICE

A. Read the following paragraph contrasting the lives of apartment
dwellers and house residents. Then write the answers to the
questions.

Apartment dwellers and house residents have different lives. Unlike house residents, apartment dwellers usually know only a few of their neighbors. House residents may have to do some maintenance, but the superintendent or building manager usually takes care of repairs in an apartment building. Although house residents are reasonably safe once they are home, apartment dwellers may be attacked by muggers hiding in elevators and stairwells. While house residents may value safety first, some apartment dwellers value convenience to shopping, day care, and health facilities more than safety.

1. What signal words tell you that the writer is making a contrast?

   _____ _____ _____ _____ _____

2. What differences does the writer point out?

   _____

   _____

3. Who is mentioned first in each point of contrast?

   _____

4. Why is it important for the writer to keep the same order?

   _____

B. This paragraph points out some differences between careful people and careless people. However, it needs signal words to make the differences clearer. In each blank space, write a word that signals contrast. Use some of the signal words listed earlier in this chapter.

The first signal word has been inserted for you. When you have finished, reread the paragraph to make sure the contrasts make sense.

Careful people and careless people differ in their attitudes towards accidents. A careful person knows accidents can happen to anybody, *whereas* a careless person thinks accidents only happen to other people. A careful person never smokes in bed. _____ a careless person may start a serious fire after falling asleep with a lit cigarette. A careful person prevents hot spills by turning pot handles toward the center or back of the stove. A careless person _____ may let pot handles extend outwards. A careful person stores paint, chemicals, and medicines out of children's reach. _____ a careless person might not think of the dangers of poisons.

C. Write a paragraph of contrast. Select a topic from the following list, or choose a topic of your own. Use the prewriting instructions in Chapters 1–5 to help you prepare. Then write your rough draft and revise it so that the supporting sentences explain what you stated in your topic sentence.

how my new supervisor is different from the one I used to have

how the U.S. differs from the Dominican Republic (or any place you know about outside the U.S.), or how your state differs from another state in the U.S.

how my new record player differs from my old one

how the lifestyles of teenagers and adults are different

How Sonny (or Tubbs) and their boss, the police lieutenant, are different in attitude and behavior (you can choose any two other contrasting characters from TV shows you like)

how two stars (in sports, movies, TV, or music) I admire are different

two political leaders who are not alike

people who are in their twenties and teenagers

how I think stars and ordinary people are not alike in their lives

how rural areas and urban areas are different

how the place where I lived (or worked) before I came to the U.S. is different from the place where I live (or work) now in the U.S.

how clubs for older people and younger people are different

two different animals I hunt (or two kinds of fish I fish for)

two different designs for a piece of carpentry (or other crafts work)

two different pets I have had

fancy clothes and everyday clothes

two different models of the same machine that I have used

summer clothes and winter clothes

TV with a VCR (or cable TV) and TV without a VCR (or cable TV)

motorcycles and bicycles

Lesson 4   WRITING A PARAGRAPH OF COMPARISON

A paragraph of comparison explains the similarity, or sameness, of two people, places, things, or ideas, such as the following:

People: two similar friends, two (boy-or-girl) friends who are alike, two stars who are alike (in music, movies, TV, sports), two politicians who are alike, two similar supervisors or bosses, two similar coworkers, two similar store owners

Places: two similar workplaces, two similar apartments or houses where I have lived, two similar places where I have spent my vacation, two similar department stores, discount stores and department stores, bus stations and train (or subway) stations

Things: two similar diets, two similar recipes, two similar cars, two similar pieces of handcraft I have made, two similar magazines (or newspaper columns) I like to read, two similar pet cats (or dogs), two similar animals I hunt (or fish that I fish for), two similar dresses (or men's suits) I have, typewriters and computers, two models of the same machine that I use, two similar brand-name products

Ideas: ideas of right and wrong I share with my parents or friends, political ideas I share with my family or friends, religious beliefs I share with my family and friends, ideas of what is good in music, movies, sports, political leadership that I share with my family or friends

The topic sentence in a paragraph of comparison states what is alike and lets the reader knows that an explanation of the similarities will follow. For the topic, *the similarities between an egg roll and a burrito*, the topic sentence is *An egg roll and a burrito are alike in many ways*. The purpose is to explain. The writer will compare size, wrapping, insides, and cooking methods.

> **An egg roll and a burrito are alike in many ways.**
> They are about the same size. Both the egg roll and the burrito have an outer layer, or wrapping, made of flour. Each contains chopped meats and vegetables. The egg roll and the burrito are cooked similarly. They are deep-fried to a crisp golden brown.

Notice that when both the egg roll and burrito are named, the egg roll is always named first. Using the same order each time makes the comparison easy to understand.

Lesson 5   USING WORDS THAT SIGNAL COMPARISON

Signal words help make the writer's meaning clear to the reader. Look for words in the paragraph about the egg roll and the burrito that signal comparison.

The writer used the signal words **alike, same, both,** and **similarly.** These and other words in the list at the beginning of this chapter are used to tell the truth that the paragraph will be describing similarities.

The next paragraph of comparison about Joe and Steve uses some comparison signal words. The topic sentence and signal words are shown in boldface.

> **Joe and Steve are alike enough to be twins.** They are **equally** tall. **Both** Joe and Steve have broad, muscular shoulders. The two of them even smile **in the same way.** They **also** have many **common** interests, such as photography and sports. Joe accepts people the way they are. Likewise, Steve is friendly to everyone.

Signal words highlight similarities between Joe and Steve. In this way, they make the comparisons clearer.

PRACTICE

A. Read the following paragraph of comparison about the way a father is raising his son. Then write the answers to the questions.

> Julio is raising his son Juan in the same way that Julio himself was raised. Just as Julio's parents brought him up to work hard but to enjoy himself, so he is teaching Juan to do his homework regularly and to have a social life. As a boy, Julio learned about his family's history from his father's stories. Likewise, Juan is gaining a feeling for his family tradition by listening to his father tell about their ancestors. Both father and son share a common love of music. Julio played the guitar for Juan when his son was little. Similarly, Juan now entertains his friends and family by playing the electric guitar in a band.

1. What signal words tell you that the writer is making comparisons?

   _____ _____ _____ _____

2. What similarities does the writer point out?

   _____
   _____
   _____

3. Who is mentioned first in each point of comparison?

_____

4. Why is it important for the writer to keep the same order?

_____

B. This paragraph of comparison is about the similarities between two people's systems of paying bills. However, it needs signal words to make the similarities clear. In each blank space, write a word that signals comparison. Use words from the list on the first page of this chapter. The first signal word has been inserted for you. When you have finished, reread the paragraph to make sure the comparisons make sense.

> **The systems that Larry and Gina use to pay bills are alike.** Larry puts his bills in a folder marked To Pay. Gina does _likewise_ Larry's folder contains four envelopes, marked Rent, Phone, Utilities, and Medical. Gina's folder is _____ organized. After Larry pays a bill, he writes on it PAID, the date, and whether he paid with a money order, a check, or cash. Gina writes _____ kind of information on her bills. _____ people keep accurate records.

C. Write a paragraph of comparison. Select a topic from the following list or from the list of topics on pages 105–106. You can also choose a topic of your own. Use the prewriting instructions in Chapters 1–5 to help you prepare. Then write your rough draft and revise it so that the supporting sentences explain what you stated in your topic sentence.

> the similarities between my best friend and her sister
>
> how my town (or neighborhood) and the next town (or neighbor-hood) are similar
>
> how the bus and train are alike
>
> what both my friends and I like to do for fun
>
> two similar main characters on two TV shows I like
>
> two sports stars whose playing styles are similar

Student Assignment

Revise your rough drafts (paragraphs of comparison and contrast) to improve their organization and use of signal words.

Revising Checklist

After you have revised each rough draft, discuss it with your teacher or another person. Use the checklist as a guide.

1. Does my topic sentence indicate that I will be explaining similarities (differences)?
2. Did I include only similarities in my paragraph of comparison?
3. Did I include only differences in my paragraph of contrast?
4. Did I rearrange the order of my sentences to make the meaning clear?
5. Did I use any signal words in order to make my meaning clearer?
6. Did I always name the same first point in the series of comparisons or contrasts in my paragraph?

Video Replay

In the video, Tony is upset that the product he received did not match his expectations. Have you ever bought a product that didn't work properly? What did you do? Write about your experience. Share your writing with another person.

ON YOUR OWN

12 REVISING FOR ORGANIZATION

Spatial Order

VIDEO FOCUS

In the video, Mrs. G. revises a letter that describes her new home. Paula, a coworker, helps her with the revision. Mrs. G. tells how the rooms are arranged in relation to each other, floor by floor. She organizes her ideas in **spatial order**.

Describing how something looks is like drawing a picture with words. A reader gets a mental image of what the writing is about. The more lively and detailed the description is, the more the reader can "see" what the writer sees.

Chapter Objectives

After seeing the video and completing this chapter, you will understand how to

- tell if you should organize your ideas in spatial order
- identify the position of one thing in relation to another in space
- write and revise a paragraph organized according to spatial order
- use words that make spatial order seem clear.

Key Words

Here are some important words that appear in this chapter or on the video. Notice how they are used. If you come across a word that is not on the list, write it down and ask your teacher to explain it.

spatial order

Signal Words

above, on top of, upon, over
below, on the bottom of, beneath, under
between, among
in the middle of, in the center of
beside, next to

left (right)
in back (front) of, behind
east, west, north, south
around, surrounding
opposite

Lesson 1 ORGANIZING DESCRIPTION OF APPEARANCE OR LOCATION IN SPATIAL ORDER

In the video, Mrs. G. revises her description of her house. The organization of the revised paragraph makes it easier to picture what the house looks like.

When writers describe the appearance or location of a person, a place, or a thing, they arrange the details in spatial order. **Spatial order** refers to the position of things in space. Organizing according to spatial order helps the reader "see" what is being described.

To decide whether you should organize your ideas in spatial order, ask yourself these questions about your rough draft:

1. Is my *writing purpose* to describe the appearance or location in space of a person, place, or thing?

2. Would my *meaning* be clearer if I organized my description in spatial order?

3. Would the sentences in the paragraph *support* the topic sentence better if they were organized according to spatial order?

In this descriptive paragraph, the details are organized in spatial order. The topic is *the appearance of the diner where I eat lunch*. The writing purpose is to describe. The topic and writing purpose are expressed in the topic sentence, which is shown in boldface.

> **The diner where I eat lunch is laid out very efficiently.** In front is the lunch counter, which has fifteen stools. Behind the counter are the coffee urns, soda dispenser, dishes, and silverware trays. Sandwiches are made in the area to the left of the coffee urns. Six booths are along the wall opposite the sandwich-making area. While the waitress is making sandwiches, she can see what the customers in the booths will be needing next.

The topic sentence is followed by the first supporting sentence, which tells the reader that the description will begin in the front of the diner, at the counter. Each detail is then presented in relation to the previous detail. The supporting sentences move from the counter itself to the area behind the counter to the left of this area. The paragraph ends with the booths along the wall opposite the sandwich-making area.

Because the writer began in front with the counter and moved in a logical and orderly way to the other areas, the reader should find it easy to picture the appearance of the diner. He or she ought to be able to sketch the location of each area described.

Lesson 2   USING WORDS THAT SIGNAL SPATIAL ORDER

Signal words help the writer move from one idea to the next in a paragraph. They also help the reader identify the way the paragraph is organized. Look for words in the paragraph about the diner that help you see how it looks.

The writer used the signal words **in front, behind, left**, and **opposite**. These and other words on the list at the beginning of the chapter are used to signal the relationship of details (people, places, or things) to each other in space. By arranging details in spatial order and using signal words effectively, you help the reader see what you are describing.

The next descriptive paragraph uses some of these signal words. The topic sentence and the signal words are shown in boldface.

> **The hot fudge sundae looked delicious.** A red maraschino cherry sat **at the top. Surrounding** the cherry was fresh whipped cream. A thick layer of hot fudge sauce was **under** the whipped cream. **Beneath** the hot fudge was a large scoop of vanilla ice cream.

When you use spatial order to describe things or people, it is important to decide where to begin. Your description may move in three basic directions. It may move from top to bottom or bottom to top, as in a description of a person. It may move from front to back or back to front, as in a description of a car. It may move from left to right or right to left, as in a description of a block of store fronts. Whatever direction you choose, be sure that you use signal words effectively to help the reader "see" what you see.

A. The following sentences support the topic sentence, **From the top shelf to the bottom shelf, the laundry store room was a mess.** However, they do not list the details in any clear spatial order. First, organize the details in spatial order from top to bottom by numbering them. The first detail has been done for you. Then organize them into another paragraph from bottom to top by numbering them. When you have finished, reread the topic sentence and the supporting sentences to make sure your organization makes sense.

_____ Half-empty boxes of detergent, dirty sponges, and coat hangers were dumped on the third shelf.

_____ On the second shelf, rolls of toilet paper were mixed with the cleaning supplies and light bulbs.

_1_ On the top shelf, piles of unfolded towels, pillow cases, and sheets were thrown together.

_____ Used gum wrappers, dirty tissue, and pieces of lint covered the bottom shelf.

B. Repeat Exercise A with the next group of sentences. They describe people on a park bench. First, organize the supporting sentences so that they describe the scene from right to left. The first sentence has been done for you. Then organize the details into another paragraph describing the scene from left to right.

From one end of the long park bench to the other, a variety of people sunned themselves.

_____ On the left, an elderly couple read the newspaper.

_1_ On the right was a mother watching her baby as he toddled on the grass.

_____ In the middle, a man sat listening to music on a portable radio.

C. This paragraph describes the appearance of a receptionist's desk. It needs signal words to help the reader understand how the desk looks. In each blank space, write a signal word that makes the description clear. Use two or three signal words: **on the left side, on the right side of, next to**, and **beside**. The first signal word has been inserted for you. When you have finished, reread the paragraph to make sure your organization makes sense.

The receptionist's desk was neat and well-organized from the left side to the right. On the left side sat the telephone switchboard, with buttons for the different offices. _____ the telephone was the daily appointment book with the names of people scheduled for interviews. _____ the appointment book was a small pad on which the receptionist wrote messages. A small vase of yellow and purple flowers sat _____ the desk.

After you have finished, share you description with someone. After the person reads it, ask him or her to draw a simple picture of what you have described. See if your reader got the picture you wanted to communicate.

D. This paragraph is meant to describe a dog from his nose to his tail (front to back), but the details are not in correct order. Read the paragraph. Then revise it. The topic sentence (shown in boldface), should come first. Then arrange the details from front to back. Picture a dog in your mind as you reorganize, since no signal words are here to help you. When you have finished, reread the paragraph to make sure your organization makes sense.

1. Sid introduced us to his new dog, Shep. 2. Between Shep's neck and tail, his coat had curly, black-and-white patches of hair. **3.** One side of Shep's face was white, and the other side was black. **4.** Shep's short black tail wagged whenever we petted him and called him "good boy." **5.** Shep had a big, black nose, which was wet and cold.

REVIEW EXERCISES

1. Describe one of the characters from any of the videos from top to bottom using spatial order. Share your description with another student and see if they recognize the person you have described.

2. Write a description of a person, place, or thing in a photograph you have. Organize your writing according to one of the patterns of spatial order. Have someone read your description, or read it aloud to one or more people. Then show your audience the photo. Have them tell you what they saw—and did not see—from your description. Ask them what you could add or change to make your written picture clearer.

Student Assignment

If you wrote a paragraph that describes the appearance or location of a person, place, or a thing, revise your rough draft to improve its organization and use of signal words.

If you do not have a rough draft of this kind of paragraph this would be a good opportunity to try writing one. Describe one of the items from the following list or choose your own topic. Use the prewriting instructions in Chapters 1–5 to help you prepare to write. Then write your rough draft and revise it so that the description moves in one direction from one detail to the next.

Topics for a Paragraph Showing Spatial Order

People	*Places*	*Things (and Animals)*
family member	a record store	a tool
best friend	a playground	a car
favorite teacher	a park, or a gym	a pet
religious or	church/synagogue	a piece of clothing, or
political	a supermarket	weaving, or carpentry
leader	a workplace	a television set
movie (or TV)	a movie theater	a hunting rifle or fishing rod
star	your home	a piece of sports equipment
favorite singer		a machine you use
employer		
sports star		

Try describing the people from top to bottom. Describe the places from front to back or side to side. Describe the things from front to back, top to bottom, or side to side.

Revising Checklist

After you have revised your paragraph, discuss your work with your teacher or another person. Use the checklist as a guide.

1. Does my topic sentence indicate that I will be describing a person, a place, or a thing?

2. Did I rearrange my sentences to make the spatial order clear?

3. Does my description move in one direction such as from front to back, left to right, or top to bottom?

4. Did I add or change any signal words in order to make the spatial order clear?

Video Replay

In the video, Mrs. G. revised her description of her new house. Describe the place where you live, or a place where you used to live, or a place where you would like to live. Share your description with another person.

UNIT 3

REVISING FOR STYLE

DEVELOPING YOUR WRITING STYLE

Everyone has his or her own way of speaking, dressing, and acting. An individual, personal way of doing something is called a **style**. It is as characteristic of you as your fingerprint.

Each person also writes in his or her own particular way. When you write a letter to a close friend, he or she may "hear" your voice because of your sentence structures and word choices. Sentence structure—the way you arrange subjects and verbs in a sentence—and the words you use are the two basic tools for creating a style.

When you revise your writing for style, you also try to make your writing as interesting as possible for the reader. Starting sentences in the same way over and over, or writing too many short sentences, usually produces a boring style. To avoid doing this, writers **vary**, or change, their sentence beginnings and the lengths of their sentences. Varying their sentences in these two ways gives their style **variety**—the characteristic of always changing, of always being different. By these revisions writers give their writing variety of **rhythm**—that is, the way their sentences move and sound keeps changing, the way the beat of a piece of music might keep changing.

You also will learn in this unit how to improve your style by avoiding the use of dull, general words, words we say all the time, such as *good, nice, great*. You will learn to choose the kind of language that will be appropriate for your audience, too. By selecting your words carefully and keeping in mind the reader you are writing for, you will use the type of language that will communicate your meaning most clearly and make the best possible impression.

ON YOUR OWN

CHAPTER *13*

Varying Sentence Lengths

VIDEO FOCUS

In the video, Maria helps Jolene revise her letter to a Legal Aid lawyer. The letter sounds stiff and choppy because it contains too many short sentences. Maria shows Jolene how to make some of her sentences longer by combining two sentences.

Combining short sentences makes writing flow more smoothly. A piece of writing that contains both long and short sentences has an interesting rhythm.

Chapter Objectives

After seeing the video and completing this chapter, you will understand how to vary sentence lengths by

- combining a sentence with another sentence to show a time relationship
- combining a sentence with another sentence to show a cause-and-effect relationship
- combining a sentence with another sentence using a connector
- adding information to the end of a sentence.

Key Words

Some words that help writers vary sentence lengths are listed on the next page. Listen for them in the video and look for them in the chapter to see how they are used.

style	**Time words:** before, after, when, as, while
vary, variety	**Cause-and-effect words:** because, if, since
rhythm	**Connectors:** and, but, yet, so, or

WHY YOU SHOULD VARY SENTENCE LENGTHS

When you talk, your sentences are usually of different lengths. If the sentences you spoke were all the same length, the rhythm of your speech would sound boring and mechanical. When you write, therefore, you want to use a variety of long and short sentences so that your writing will be interesting and alive.

A paragraph may have a choppy rhythm because it contains several short sentences in a row. In the video, Jolene's letter sounded choppy and boring for this reason. You can revise a paragraph by expanding or combining some of the sentences. This chapter shows you four ways to revise paragraphs with too many short sentences.

Lesson 1   COMBINING SHORT SENTENCES THAT SHOW TIME RELATIONSHIPS

In the video, Jolene revises her letter to improve her style by combining two of the many short sentences in it. In her writing, she gives a history of what happened between herself and her old landlord when she moved. Because she is writing about events in time, she combines the sentences into a longer sentence by using **before** and **since**—two connecting words that show a time relationship. When short sentences show time relationships, you can combine them by using one of the following words: *before, since, when, after, as*, and *while*. Be sure the word you choose accurately describes *when* or *the order in which* the events occurred. The time word is in boldface in the following examples:

Their old lease expired. They already were eager to move.
Before their old lease expired, they already were eager to move.

They began looking for a new home. They had found nothing they liked.
Since they began looking for a new home, they had found nothing they liked.

They saw a house for rent. It was being painted.
When they saw a house for rent, it was being painted.

They read the lease slowly. The new landlord waited impatiently.
As they read the lease slowly, the new landlord waited
impatiently.

They signed the lease. Everyone was satisfied.
After they signed the lease, everyone was satisfied.

They drove home. Music played softly on the car radio.
While they drove home, music played softly on the car radio.

Notice in the preceding examples that when you use a time word to combine short sentences, you put a comma before the second part of the revised sentence.

PRACTICE

Revise the following paragraph. Combine each pair of short sentences using the time words at the end of each pair. Make sure you add a comma before the second part of the revised sentence. The first pair has been combined for you. When you have finished, read the revised paragraph aloud to hear the difference in rhythm. Be sure your combined sentences make sense.

When Augusto arrived in the laundry room, all the washing machines were empty.

1. Augusto arrived in the laundry room. All the washing machines were empty. (**when**) 2. Augusto prepared the clothes for washing. A neighbor told him how she got her high school equivalency diploma. (**while**) 3. Augusto sorted the clothes according to dark and light colors. He used stain remover on the clothes that were very dirty. (**after**) 4. The washing machine filled with water. He added the soap. (**as**) 5. Augusto placed the clothes in the machine. He closed the lid. (**after**) 6. He finished talking to his neighbor. His clothes were clean. (**before**)

Lesson 2 COMBINING SHORT SENTENCES THAT SHOW CAUSE-AND-EFFECT RELATIONSHIPS

A cause is something that makes something happen. An effect is what happens. To combine two short sentences that are related by a cause-

and-effect relationship, you can use the following connecting words: **because, since**, and **if**. For a complete list of cause-and-effect connecting words, look at the beginning of Chapter 10, which gives a fuller discussion of causes and effects in writing. All the connecting words treated in Chapter 10 are punctuated in the same way as **because, since**, and **if**. Notice in the following examples where the comma is used when the sentences are combined.

> My friends dance. I want to dance.
> **Because** my friends dance, I want to dance.

> It is cold in February. I wear heavy clothes all month long.
> **Since** it is cold in February, I wear heavy clothes all month long.

You will notice that **since** can be used as a connecting word for both time relationships and cause-and-effect relationships. When it is used as a cause-and-effect word, it means the same thing as **because**. If you cannot substitute **because** for the **since** in a sentence, then it must be **since** used as a time word.

> **Since** yesterday, she has been sad.

(You cannot write, "Because yesterday, she has been sad," so the *since* is a time word.)

> **Since** it snowed yesterday, my school is closed.

(You can substitute **because** for *since*, as in "Because it snowed yesterday, my school is closed," so *since* is a cause-and-effect word in this sentence.)

> We go to the movies early. We get a good seat.
> **If** we go to the movies early, we get a good seat.

Remember, when you use a cause-and-effect word to combine short sentences, add a comma before the second part of the revised sentence. Read the revised sentence to make sure it makes sense.

PRACTICE

Revise the following paragraph. Combine each pair of short sentences by using the cause-and-effect word at the end of each pair of sentences. Remember to add the comma before the second part of the revised sentence. The first pair has been combined for you. When you have finished, read the revised paragraph aloud so that you can hear the differences in rhythm. Be sure your combined sentences make sense. The first pair of sentences has been done for you.

Yuriko was lonely, **because** she was new in town and did not know many people.

1. Yuriko was lonely. She was new in town and did not know many people. (**because**) 2. The town was small. Almost everyone knew each other. (**since**) 3. She introduced herself to her neighbors. She would make new friends. (**if**) 4. She made new friends quickly. Her neighbors knew her family. (**because**)

Lesson 3 COMBINING SHORT SENTENCES USING *AND*, *BUT, YET, SO*, AND *OR*

And, but, yet, so, and **or** can be used to connect sentences. The word you use depends on the meaning you want. Here are two kinds of connections you can make with these words. The connecting words, or connectors, are shown in boldface.

1. *Combining short sentences that have the same subject.*

Make sure that the revised sentence makes sense.

Jose visited his uncle. Jose wrote to his friend.
Jose visited his uncle **and** wrote to his friend.

Jose spent the day with his uncle. Jose then went to work.
Jose spent the day with his uncle **but** then went to work.

Jose's uncle could take a walk. Jose's uncle could eat dinner.
Jose's uncle could take a walk **or** eat dinner.

2. *Combining short sentences that have different subjects.*

The connectors **and, but, yet, so,** and **or** can be used to combine two short related sentences. A comma is used before the connector to show where the original first sentence ends. When you use these words, be sure the revised sentence makes sense.

> Kim ate stir-fried vegetables for dinner. Manuel ate beef stew.

> Kim ate stir-fried vegetables for dinner, **and** Manual ate beef stew.

> Kim loved vegetables. Manual didn't.
> Kim loved vegetables, **but** Manuel didn't.

> Kim and Manuel like to eat out. They cannot afford to very often.
> Kim and Manuel like to eat out, **yet** they cannot afford to very often.

> Kim and Manuel finished eating late. They went straight home.
> Kim and Manuel finished eating late, **so** they went straight home.

> Kim and Manuel could eat together. They could eat separately.
> Kim and Manuel could eat together, **or** they could eat separately.

PRACTICE

A. Revise the following paragraph. Combine each pair of short sentences by using the connector shown at the end of each pair. The first pair of sentences has been combined for you. When you have finished, read the revised paragraph aloud to hear the difference in rhythm.

1. The supervisor promoted Betsy **and** fired Annette.

1. The supervisor promoted Betsy. He fired Annette. (**and**) **2.** Betsy was proud of herself. She felt badly for Annette. (**but**) **3.** She decided she would rather find another job. She left the same day. (**so**) **4.** Annette could appeal the supervisor's decision. She could accept it. (**or**)

B. Revise the following paragraph. Combine each pair of short sentences by using the connecting word shown at the end of each pair. Remember to use a comma when it is needed. The first pair of sentences has been combined for you. When you have finished, read the revised paragraph aloud to hear the difference in rhythm.

> **1.** Leonardo drives a city bus**, and** his wife Laura drives a school bus.

> **1.** Leonardo drives a city bus. His wife Laura drives a school bus. (**and**) **2.** Leonardo recognizes his regular riders. Laura knows all of the children by name. (**but**) **3.** Both of their driving jobs are exhausting. They love their work. (**yet**) **4.** Leonardo and Laura work on their house at night. They watch television. (**or**) **5.** They work long days. They go to bed early. (**so**)

Lesson 4 ADDING INFORMATION AT THE END OF SHORT SENTENCES

Read the following paragraph aloud. Notice how choppy the four short sentences sound.

> Scott works in a hardware store. He organizes the carpentry supplies. He also sets up displays of drills. He dusts and sweeps.

Here is the same paragraph with information added to the end of the sentence. The new information is shown in boldface. What would you say is the difference in rhythm? Does the paragraph seem more interesting now?

> Scott works in a hardware store **as a clerk**. He organizes the carpentry supplies **such as nuts, bolts, and nails**. He also sets up displays of drills **in the store window**. He dusts and sweeps **at the end of the day**.

The added information tells *what kind* of job Scott had, gives *examples* of the carpentry supplies, tells *where* Scott set up the drill display, and tells *when* he dusted and swept. What kind of information would you have added to the paragraph? When you add information to the end of short sentences, you can make your writing more informative and interesting.

Read this choppy paragraph aloud. Do not read the words in parentheses. Revise the paragraph by adding the information asked for in the parentheses. The first sentence has been done for you. Notice that the added information, *every day*, tells *when*. Remember, there is more than one way to tell *when*. For instance, you might have written *three times a day* instead of *every day*. When you have finished, read the revised paragraph aloud to hear the difference in rhythm.

Good nutrition means eating sensibly **every day**.

Good nutrition means eating sensibly (**when**). Eat healthy foods (**such as**). Avoid using too much sugar and salt (**in what**). Also, cut down on food with lots of fat and cholesterol. If you drink alcohol, set a daily limit of one or two drinks (**what kind**).

REVIEW EXERCISES

A. Revise the following paragraph. Combine each pair of short sentences using the word after each pair of sentences. The words may be connectors, show time relationships, or show cause-and-effect relationships. The first pair has been combined for you. Remember to add the comma where it is needed. After you have finished, read the revised paragraph aloud to hear the difference in rhythm. Be sure the revised paragraph makes sense.

Before I filled out the tax form, I read the instructions.

1. I filled out the tax form. I read the instructions. (**before**) 2. Someone else used to prepare my taxes. I was afraid I couldn't do my taxes without making a mistake. (**because**) 3. I took the GED course. Now I am willing to try things that were once too hard for me. (**and**) 4. My brother checked my work. I worked through the whole tax form. (**as**) 5. I mailed in my completed tax forms with a request for a refund. I was finished. (**when**)

B. Revise the following paragraph by combining sentences that have a time relationship. Use some of these time words: **when, as, after, before, while**. When you have finished, read the revised paragraph so that you can hear the difference your revisions have made in the rhythms of the sentences. Be sure the revisions all make sense.

> Elaine had a very painful stomach infection. She finally went into the hospital. She got out of the hospital. Her doctor told her to get lots of rest. Elaine went home. Her friends came to visit her. She told them about her doctor's advice. They listened carefully. Elaine rested on the sofa. Her friends cooked dinner for her. She ate dinner with them. She went to bed.

C. Revise the following paragraph. Combine sentences that have a cause-and-effect relationship by using **because, if**, and **since**. When you have finished, read the revised paragraph aloud to hear the difference in rhythm. Be sure the revised paragraph makes sense.

> You can prevent a young child from choking. Keep tiny objects, broken toys, and toys with small parts out of an infant's reach. Infants like to put things into their mouths. Children run while they are eating. They can choke on their food. Sitting down to eat will help teach them table manners. You can teach them to feed themselves properly.

D. Revise the following paragraph by varying the sentence lengths. You may add information to the end of the sentences, or you may combine short sentences. Remember that you can combine sentences by using words that are connectors, or that show time relationships, or that show cause-and-effect relationships. When you have finished, read the revised paragraph aloud so that you can hear the variety of rhythms your revisions have created. Be sure the revised paragraph makes sense. The topic sentence (in boldface) should stay separate.

> **Employees are fired from their jobs for many reasons.** They come to work late or they leave early. Their boss lets them go. An employee is rude to coworkers. He may be fired. One woman employee ignored phone calls from a customer. She lost her job. Some employees produce poor-quality work. They do not hold any job for long. Others place their fellow workers in danger. They ignore safety rules. Certain employees work too slowly. Their jobs aren't finished on time and others have to work overtime to finish them.

Student Assignment

If you have a rough draft of your own that you are revising, look at it now to see if varying sentence lengths would make it more interesting.

If you don't have a rough draft, try writing one. Use the prewriting and drafting instructions in Chapters 1–6. Then revise your draft for organization (see Chapters 7–12). Finally, revise it for variety in sentence length.

Revising Checklist

Read aloud your revised paragraph or a paragraph you revised in Review Exercises B, C, or D. Discuss your writing with your teacher or another person. Use the following checklist as a guide.

1. Did I write sentences of different lengths?
2. Did I add information to the end of some short sentences?
3. Did I combine some sentences using the connecting words *and, but, yet, so*, and *or*?
4. Did I combine some sentences that show time relationships?
5. Did I combine some sentences that show cause-and-effect relationships?
6. Is the rhythm of the paragraph more interesting as a result of the revisions?

Video Replay

In the video, Jolene revises a letter asking for legal help. She wants to make her landlord return her security deposit. Have you ever had a problem getting a refund of your money? Write about your experience and share your writing with another person.

ON YOUR OWN

14 REVISING FOR STYLE

Varying Sentence Beginnings

VIDEO FOCUS

In the video, Jerry helps his wife Connie revise her friend Kathy's letter about child custody. The letter tells why Kathy thinks the children's father should not have custody. Although the information in the letter is accurate, the rhythm and wording of the sentences are repetitious. Three sentences begin with the same subject and verb. If Kathy uses different sentence beginnings, her letter will make a better impression.

Starting sentences in different ways keeps them from sounding the same and gives them different rhythms. It makes the sentences flow more smoothly and keeps them from being boring. Varying sentence beginnings gives variety to your writing, which will make it more interesting for your reader.

Chapter Objectives

After seeing the video and completing this chapter, you will understand how to

- move phrases that tell *when* or *where* to the beginning of the sentence
- reverse the order of clauses that show time relationship
- reverse the order of clauses that show cause-and-effect relationships.

Here are some important words and phrases that appear in this chapter or on the video. Notice how they are used. If you come across a new word that is not on this list, write it down and ask your teacher to explain it.

phrase   clause
when phrase   dependent clause
where phrase   independent clause

REVERSING THE ORDER OF PHRASES TO VARY SENTENCE BEGINNINGS

Phrases are groups of words that lack a subject or a verb, or lack both. They are used in sentences to add information or description. Phrases tell *when* something happens or *where* something is located. For example, look at theses examples:

After a tiring week

Next to the kitchen

In these two word groups, what action is taking place? Who has had a tiring week? What is located next to the kitchen? It is impossible to answer these questions. The first word group tells only *when* someone did or felt something, not *who* had a tiring week, or what happened. The second word group tells only *where* something is located, not *what* that thing is, or what happened. Neither group of words has a subject or a verb. They are not complete sentences. They are phrases.

You can vary the way a sentence starts by moving phrases that tell *when* or *where* to the beginning of the sentence. Beginning some sentences with these kinds of phrases makes the writing more interesting to read.

Lesson 1   MOVING PHRASES THAT TELL *WHEN* TO THE BEGINNING OF THE SENTENCE

Read the following paragraph aloud. Notice that all the sentences begin repetitiously with the subject. The **when phrase**, the phrase telling *when* (shown in boldface), is always at the end of the sentence.

All Jeff wanted to do was sleep **after a tiring week**. He went to bed early **on Friday night**. He felt rested **by Saturday morning**. Jeff answered two help wanted ads **before eating lunch**. He helped his friends Virginia and Tom paint their house **in the afternoon**. Jeff and his wife visited friends **in the evening**.

The revised paragraph is as follows, with some of the phrases moved to the beginnings of their sentences. These phrases which were moved are shown in boldface. Notice that when you move a phrase with at least three words to the beginning of the sentence, you put a comma after it.

After you have made the changes, read the paragraph aloud. Although the ideas have not changed, the paragraph will have a more interesting rhythm, because some of the sentences begin with a phrase.

> **After a tiring week**, all Jeff wanted to do was sleep. He went to bed early on Friday night. **By Saturday morning**, he felt rested. Jeff answered two help wanted ads before eating lunch. **In the afternoon**, he helped his friends Virginia and Tom paint their house. Jeff and his wife visited friends in the evening.

Lesson 2   MOVING PHRASES THAT TELL *WHERE* TO THE BEGINNING OF THE SENTENCE

Read the following paragraph aloud. Notice that all the sentences begin repetitiously with the subject. The **where phrase**, the phrase telling *where* (shown in boldface), is always at the end of the sentence.

> Jeff's wife needed some tools to put up shelves. Jeff gave her the following directions about where the toolbox was. You will find a closet with three shelves **next to the kitchen**. I have stored things to do with home repair **on the top shelf**. Washers and other small plumbing supplies are in boxes **in the middle of this shelf**. Several rolls of electrical tape are in paper bags **to the left of the plumbing supplies**. You will see a red metal box with a handle **behind the electrical tape**. That is the toolbox.

The revised paragraph is as follows. The phrases that have been moved to the beginning of the sentence are shown in boldface. Read the paragraph aloud. Although the ideas haven't been changed, the paragraph is more interesting to read, because some sentences begin with a phrase. Notice that a comma is used at the end of a phrase with at least three words when it begins a sentence.

> Jeff's wife needed some tools to put up shelves. Jeff gave her the following directions about where the toolbox was. **Next to the kitchen**, you will find a closet with three shelves. I have stored things to do with home repair on the

top shelf. **In the middle of the shelf,** washers and other small plumbing supplies are in boxes. Several rolls of electrical tape are in paper bags to the left of the plumbing supplies. **Behind the electrical tape,** you will see a red metal box with a handle. That is the toolbox.

PRACTICE

Read the following paragraph. Notice that it contains five phrases which are in boldface. Move three of the phrases to the beginning of their sentences. The second sentence has been revised for you. Notice that when you move a phrase with at least three words to the beginning of the sentence, you put a comma after it.

After you have made the changes, read the paragraph aloud. Although the ideas have not changed, the paragraph will have a more interesting rhythm, because some of the sentences begin with a phrase.

Usual Order: Feelings such as anger and loneliness can be especially strong **at the end of the day**.

Revised Order: **At the end of the day,** feelings such as anger and loneliness can be especially strong.

Many people in emotional pain abuse food, alcohol, or drugs **at night**. Feelings such as anger and loneliness can be especially strong **at the end of the day**. People hope that what they eat, drink, or inject will help them fall asleep. They usually feel worse **in the morning**. They take more of their substance **during the night**. The problems get worse. Most people must fully experience the hopelessness of their situation **before accepting help from support groups.**

Read the following paragraph. Notice that the paragraph contains five **where phrases**, which are in boldface. Move three of the phrases to the beginnings of their sentences. One of the sentences has been revised for you. Notice that when you move a phrase with at least three words to the beginning of the sentence, you put a comma after it.

After you have revised the sentence, read the paragraph aloud. Although the ideas have not changed, the writing should have more interesting rhythms, because some sentences begin with phrases.

Usual Order: I put the sofa **right next to the front door**.
Revised Order: **Right next to the front door,** I put the sofa.

I described how I arranged my living room furniture to my friends. I put the sofa **right next to the front door**. A table with a bowl of flowers stands **on the other side of the door**. I placed my favorite rocking chair **across the room from the table**. There is a picture of my family **above my armchair**. I can look into the kitchen **from this armchair**.

REVERSING THE ORDER OF CLAUSES TO VARY SENTENCE BEGINNINGS

When you write, some of your sentences may have two parts. Each part will be expressed in a clause. You can vary your sentence beginnings by reversing the order of the clauses.

A **clause** is a group of words that has a subject and a verb. An **independent clause** expresses a complete thought and can stand alone.

> May and Frank fell in love.

A **dependent clause** is a group of words that has a subject and a verb but does not express a complete thought.

> When they first met

This clause leaves us with questions: Who met? What happened when they met? If we combine it with an independent clause, however, we can understand it.

> May and Frank fell in love **when they first met**.

A dependent clause **depends** on an independent clause in a sentence to complete its meaning. A dependent clause adds information to the main meaning of a sentence. For example, **when they first met** tells us **when** May and Frank fell in love.

Lesson 3 REVERSING THE ORDER OF CLAUSES THAT EXPRESS A TIME RELATIONSHIP

One way to vary the beginnings of sentences is to move a dependent time clause from its usual place at the end of the sentence to the beginning of the sentence. Look at this example:

Usual Order: May and Frank fell in love **when they first met**.

Revised Order: **When they first met,** May and Frank fell in love.

Notice that when the time clause is moved to the beginning of the sentence, a comma must come after it.

In the following paragraph, the sentences follow the usual order—the time clauses (shown in boldface) come at the ends of the sentences. Read the paragraph aloud, and notice how repetitious the sentences are.

> May and Frank fell in love **when they first met**. They wanted to get married **after dating a few times**. They discovered they disagreed about some important things **as they discussed their ideas about marriage**. They therefore delayed the wedding. They got premarital counseling **while they worked to understand each other better**. May and Frank have grown to love each other more **since they began talking with their minister**. They now plan to marry in six months.

In the revised paragraph, some of the time clauses have been moved from their usual place at the end of the sentence to the beginning of the sentence. Only the clauses which have been moved are in boldface. Notice that the wording and rhythm of the writing is more interesting.

> May and Frank fell in love when they first met. They wanted to get married after dating a few times. **As they discussed their ideas about marriage,** they discovered they disagreed about some important things. They therefore delayed the wedding. **While they worked to understand each other better,** they got premarital counseling. May and Frank have grown to love each other more since they began talking with their minister. They now plan to marry in six months.

Lesson 4   REVERSING THE ORDER OF CLAUSES THAT EXPRESS A CAUSE-AND-EFFECT RELATIONSHIP

Another kind of dependent clause you can use to vary sentence beginnings is a clause that explains why something happens, or why something is the way it is—a cause-and-effect clause. Like the time clauses, these dependent clauses do not express a complete thought. For example:

As a result of taking several actions...

This clause leaves us with questions: What happened because of the actions? Who did them? What actions did they take? It depends on a sentence that it is connected to for its complete meaning.

Lise and Paul have enough money to buy a house **as a result of taking several actions**.

In this sentence, the cause-and-effect clause is in its usual place at the end of the sentence. You can vary your sentence beginnings by reversing this order, like this:

Usual Order: Lise and Paul have enough money to buy a house **as a result of taking several actions**.

Revised Order: **As a result of taking several actions,** Lise and Paul have enough money to buy a house.

Notice that when the cause-and-effect clause is moved to the beginning of the sentence, a comma must come after it.

In the following paragraph, each sentence follows the usual order—the cause-and-effect (shown in boldface) comes at the end of the sentence. Read the paragraph aloud, and notice how repetitious the sentences are.

Lise and Paul will have enough money to buy a house **as a result of taking several actions**. They have more and more money in savings **because they put part of every paycheck into their savings account**. They do not withdraw money from this account **since they want to use it for a down payment on a mortgage**. They will be able to afford this mortgage soon **if they keep on saving steadily**.

In the revised paragraph, some of the cause-and-effect clauses have been moved from their usual place at the end of the sentence to the beginning of the sentence. Only the clauses which have been moved are in boldface. Notice that the wording and the rhythm of the writing is more interesting.

As a result of taking several actions, Lise and Paul will have enough money to buy a house. They have more and more money in savings because they put part of every paycheck into their savings account. **Since they want to use it for a down payment on a mortgage,** they do not withdraw money from this account. **If they keep on saving steadily,** they will be able to afford this mortgage soon.

Read the following paragraph. Notice that it contains five time clauses, which are in boldface. Move three of these clauses to the beginnings of their sentences. The second sentence has been revised for you. Be sure that when you move the clause to the beginning of the sentence, you put a comma after it. Read the revised paragraph aloud. Notice the difference in rhythm and wording.

Usual Order: You read the label **when you buy packaged food**.

Revised Order: **When you buy packaged food,** you read the label.

> You have learned how to make good choices **since the first time you shopped**. You read the label **when you buy packaged food**. You check the list of natural ingredients and additives **before you choose one of the different brands of the same product**. You think about what the product is called **while you are making your selection**. You know, for instance, that beef with gravy contains at least 50 percent cooked beef. This is more than the 35 percent cooked beef that is required in gravy with beef. You make your choice **after you read the labels of a few brands of the same product**.

Read the following paragraph. Notice it contains four cause-and-effect clauses, which are in boldface. Move two of these clauses to the beginnings of their sentences. The second sentence has been revised for you. Put a comma after the clause you move. Read the revised paragraph aloud, and notice the difference in rhythm.

Usual Order: Take it outdoors to dry **since the air in your house will hold the moisture**.

Revised Order: **Since the air in your house will hold the moisture,** take it outdoors to dry.

> Here is how to restore a wooden bureau after a flood. Take it outdoors to dry **since the air in your house will hold the moisture**. Dry the bureau in a covered area such as a garage **because direct sunlight may warp it**. It will dry faster **if you remove the drawers**. Remove the backing and push the drawers out **since you may damage them by pulling them out the front**.

A. Read the following paragraph. Notice that it contains seven phrases that tell *when* or *where*. Decide which of these phrases you want to move to the beginnings of their sentences. Read the sentences you have revised aloud to see if your changes make reading the paragraph interesting. Remember to put a comma after the phrase if you move it to the beginning of the sentence.

> Driving slowly is important **in many situations**. A car that is traveling too fast can skid **on icy roads**. The road provides less traction for car tires **during rainstorms**. It is also important to drive slowly **at night**. A cat or dog may suddenly dart in front of your car **from the left or right**. Driving slowly is necessary **on very curvy roads**. If you drive too fast, you may move into the lane on the opposite side of the road. There may be oncoming traffic **in this lane**. A serious accident could occur.

B. Read the following paragraph. Notice that it contains five clauses (shown in boldface) that express either time relationships or cause-and-effect relationships. To vary the sentence beginnings, make your own decisions on which clauses you want to move to the beginnings of their sentences. Read your revisions aloud to see if they create variety in your writing. Remember to put a comma after the clause if you move it to the beginning of a sentence.

> There are many things you can do to reduce tension. Press your fingers to your temples **when you have a headache**. Taking a walk is effective **because physical movement and fresh air usually are relaxing**. Do an activity that requires a lot of energy—such as running, waxing your floor, or washing your car **after you come home from work**. You should not consume much food or drink near bedtime **since it might disturb your sleep**. Do some gentle stretching exercises or deep-breathing **before you go to bed**.

Student Assignment

If you have a rough draft of your own that you are revising, look at it now to see if varying sentence beginnings will make it sound more interesting. If you don't have a rough draft, try writing one. Use the prewriting and drafting instructions in Chapters 1–6. Then revise your draft for organization (see Chapters 7–12). Vary sentence lengths (see Chapter 13), and revise sentence beginnings, if necessary.

Revising Checklist

Read aloud your own revised paragraph or those you revised in Review Exercises A and B. Discuss your writing with your teacher or another person. Use the checklist as a guide.

1. Did my sentences have different beginnings?

2. Did I move phrases telling when or where to the beginning of some sentences?

3. Did I reverse the order of the clauses that show a time relationship in some of the sentences?

4. Did I reverse the order of the clauses that show a cause-and-effect relationship in some of the sentences?

5. Is the rhythm of my paragraph more interesting as a result of the revisions?

Video Replay

In the video, Jerry and Connie help their friend Kathy with a personal problem by revising her letter. Write about a time when your friends helped you—or you helped friends—in dealing with a difficult situation. Share your writing with another person.

ON YOUR OWN

Untangling Confusing Sentences

VIDEO FOCUS

In the video, Blaine and Mrs. G. revise his note to some parents about a field trip. When they reread his note, they see that the meaning is confusing. The confusion occurs because one clause has been placed too far from the word it describes.

Sometimes sentences do not communicate the meaning that the writer intends because descriptive words are put in the wrong place in the sentence. The order of the words in the sentence makes the meaning confusing. The writer needs to reorder or rearrange the words to make the reader understand.

In this chapter, you will learn how to use **phrases** and **dependent clauses** to make meaning clear, or to add extra information or description. Knowing how to use them includes where to place them correctly and how to punctuate them correctly.

Chapter Objectives

After seeing the video and completing this chapter, you will understand how to

- place a phrase near the word it describes
- place a dependent clause near the word it describes
- use dependent clauses that give essential information
- use dependent clauses that give nonessential, extra information
- punctuate both kinds of dependent clauses correctly.

Key Words

Here are some important words that appear in this chapter or on the video. Notice how they are used. If you come across an unfamiliar word that does not appear on this list, write it down and ask your teacher to explain it to you.

essential dependent clause   nonessential dependent clause

Lesson 1   PLACING A PHRASE NEAR THE WORD IT DESCRIBES

In the following sentence, who had a big smile?

The woman gave the award to the girl with a big smile.

The writer intended to communicate that the *woman* had a big smile. But because the phrase, *with a big smile*, was placed closer to *girl*, the reader might think the girl had a big smile.

As you learned in Chapter 14, a **phrase** is a group of words that is not a complete sentence because it lacks a subject or a verb, or both. The following are examples of phrases:

in the blue car	holding the key
into the cafe	standing on the corner
near the bus stop	giving the child money
with a firm handshake	hitting the wall
after the storm	scared to death
by the workbench	raised by foster parents

As you saw in the preceding sentence, changing the position of a phrase in a sentence can change the meaning of the sentence. The following sentences are confusing because of where the phrase (shown in boldface) is placed.

The man **wearing the blue jacket** robbed the passenger.
(The man is wearing the blue jacket.)

The man robbed the passenger **wearing the blue jacket**.
(The passenger is wearing the blue jacket.)

In the first sentence, the phrase *wearing the blue jacket* describes *the man*. The reader knows who is wearing the blue jacket because the phrase is located next to the word *man*. In the second sentence, the phrase is placed just after the word *passenger*. Notice the difference in meaning in the second sentence. If the robber was the person wearing the blue jacket, and in your report for the police you put the phrase *wearing the blue jacket* next to the word *passenger*, you might confuse the police. The robber might get away because they would not be able to identify him.

Here is another example of how the placement of a phrase changes the meaning of a sentence.

The woman opened the door **with the key**.
(The woman used the key to open the door.)

The woman **with the key** opened the door.
(The woman who had the key was the person who opened the door.)

In the first sentence, the phrase *with the key* tells **how** the door was opened. In the second sentence, the phrase describes **who** opened the door.

The placement of phrases in a sentence is very important. Always place the phrase as close as possible to the word you want it to describe. If the phrase is not placed correctly, your message may not be clear to your reader. You, the writer, may mean one thing, but the reader may get some other meaning from your writing.

PRACTICE

Rewrite each of the following sentences by placing the phrases (shown in italics) correctly in the sentence. First, answer the question by writing the meaning you think the writer intended. Then rewrite the sentence. The first sentence has been revised for you.

1. Holdup men sometimes rob store clerks **wearing masks**.
    Meaning: (Who is wearing masks?) The holdup men are wearing masks.

    Revised: *Holdup men wearing masks sometimes rob store clerks.*

2. Smart owners buy burglar alarms from well-known companies *with loud sirens*.
    Meaning: (Who or what has loud sirens?)

    Revised: _____

3. When alarms go off during a robbery, police arrive in cars *with handguns.*
   Meaning: (Who or what has handguns?)

   Revised: _____

4. The clerks described the holdup men *with tears in their eyes.*
   Meaning: (Who had tears in their eyes?)

   Revised: _____

5. Storekeepers should use a buddy system to fight against robbers *owning nearby businesses.*
   Meaning: (Who owns nearby businesses?)

   Revised: _____

6. Citizen patrols watch out for criminals *guarding their neighborhoods.*
   Meaning: (Who is guarding the neighborhoods?)

   Revised: _____

7. Policemen sometimes instruct citizens *trained in self-defense.*
   Meaning: (Who is trained in self-defense?)

   Revised: _____

8. He was happy to see his girlfriend in his apartment *using an axe* when the police opened the door.
   Meaning: (Who was using the axe?)

   Revised: _____

9. Criminals sometimes scare working people *having shoot-outs.*
   Meaning: (Who is having shoot-outs?)

   Revised: _____

10. Drugs ruin a lot of teenagers *sold right on the street.*
    Meaning: (What or who is sold right out on the street?)

    Revised: _____

PLACING A DEPENDENT CLAUSE NEAR THE WORD IT DESCRIBES

As you learned in Chapter 14, a clause is a group of words that has a subject and a verb. A **dependent clause** depends on the rest of a sentence to make complete sense. By itself, the dependent clause does not make complete sense. In the sentence, it is used to add information to the main thought.

Lesson 2   DEPENDENT CLAUSES THAT GIVE ESSENTIAL INFORMATION

Some dependent clauses begin with **who, whom, which**, or **that**. Like phrases, dependent clauses that begin with these words should be placed near the words thy describe. In the following sentences, notice how the meaning depends on where the dependent clause (shown in boldface) is placed.

> The apartment **that was robbed** was near the store.
> (The apartment was robbed.)
>
> The apartment was near the store **that was robbed**.
> (The store was robbed.)

Notice that in the preceding examples no comma separates the dependent clause from the rest of the sentence. That is because this dependent clause gives information that is essential to the meaning of the word it describes. Therefore, it is not separated from the word with a comma. Look at the following examples of such clauses. Notice that they are placed as close as possible to the words they describe.

> The man **who attends GED classes** can help you with homework.
>
> Question: Which man can help you? The clause tells you which man: the man **who attends GED classes**.
>
> The teacher **whom everyone likes** is moving to another state.
>
> Question: Which teacher is moving? The clause tells you which teacher: the teacher **whom everyone likes**.
>
> The position **which has been advertised for only a week** is still open.
>
> Question: Which position is still open? The clause tells you which position: the position **which has been advertised for only a week**.

The city **that has the biggest population** has the worst traffic problems.

Question: Which city has the worst traffic problems? The clause tells you: the city **that has the biggest population**.

PRACTICE

Revise each of the following sentences by placing the essential dependent clauses (shown in italics) correctly. First, read the meaning the writer intended. Then revise the sentence. Remember to place the dependent clause as close as possible to the word about which it gives essential information. The first sentence has been revised for you.

1. A neighbor of mine met a real estate salesman *whom I know well*.
   Meaning: (I know the neighbor well.)

   Revised: *A real estate salesman met a neighbor of mine whom I know well.*

2. A salesman can charm a person *who feels very self-confident*.
   Meaning: (The salesman was very self-confident.)

   Revised: _____

3. The woman agreed to meet a friend of the salesman *who is my neighbor*.
   Meaning: (The woman is my neighbor.)

   Revised: _____

4. The friend of the salesman owned a large apartment near to a city park *that was vacant*.
   Meaning: (The apartment was vacant.)

   Revised: _____

5. The salesman's friend wanted a smaller apartment in place of the vacant apartment *that was furnished*.
   Meaning: (The smaller apartment would be furnished.)

   Revised: _____

6. The friend wanted another apartment in place of the vacant apartment *which was rent-controlled*.
   Meaning: (The other apartment would be rent-controlled.)

   Revised: _____

7. My neighbor had a rent-controlled apartment and did not want another apartment *that was inexpensive.*
   Meaning: (My neighbor's apartment was inexpensive.)

   Revised: _____

8. The two men wanted to take this smaller apartment of hers and give her the vacant apartment *that was rent-controlled.*
   Meaning: (Her apartment was rent-controlled.)

   Revised: _____

9. A friend told my neighbor not to sign anything with the salesman *whom she trusted.*
   Meaning: (The neighbor trusted her friend.)

   Revised: _____

10. A person like my neighbor should not deal with an expert salesman *who has no business experience.*
    Meaning: (My neighbor has no business experience.)

    Revised: _____

Lesson 3   DEPENDENT CLAUSES THAT GIVE NONESSENTIAL INFORMATION

Other dependent clauses add information that is descriptive but not essential to the meaning of the sentence. They give extra information about the words they describe. We already have the essential information about these words. Nonessential dependent clauses may begin with **who, whom, which**, and **that**. In the following sentences, examples of nonessential dependent clauses are shown in boldface. Notice that like phrases they are placed as close as possible to the words they describe.

Paul, **who attends GED classes**, needs help from the teacher.

(We already know who needs help: Paul. The clause adds the information that he attends GED classes.)

The science teacher, **whom everyone likes**, is moving to another state.

(We already know which teacher is moving: the science teacher. The clause adds the information that everyone likes her.)

The top position, **which has been advertised for only a week**, is still open.

(We already know which position is still open: the top position. The clause adds the information that it has been advertised for a week.)

Notice that all these nonessential dependent clauses are separated from the rest of the sentence with a comma or commas. If a nonessential clause comes in the middle of a sentence, commas are placed both before and after it. If it comes at the end of a sentence, a comma comes before it and a period comes after it.

Notice also that the examples above do not include a sentence using *that. That* is used only with dependent clauses that give essential information (like the "that clause" in this sentence).

PRACTICE

Revise each of the following sentences by correctly placing the non-essential dependent clause (shown in italics). First, read the meaning the writer intended. Then revise the sentence. Remember to use commas where they are necessary. The first sentence has been revised for you.

1. The driver hit the bicyclist, *who was tired from his long trip.*
   Meaning: <u>(The driver was tired.)</u>

   Revised: *The driver, who was tired from his long trip, hit the bicyclist.*

2. The driver, *who was badly shaken*, helped the bicyclist.
   Meaning: <u>(The bicyclist was badly shaken).</u>

   Revised: _____

3. The bicycle lay next to the car, *which was badly damaged.*
   Meaning: <u>(The bicycle was badly damaged.)</u>

   Revised: _____

4. The driver drove the bicyclist to the hospital in his car, *which was where he had his tonsils removed.*
   Meaning: (The hospital was where he had his tonsils removed.)

   Revised: _____

5. The nurse called the victim's family, *whom the bicyclist knew.*
   Meaning: (The bicyclist knew the nurse.)

   Revised: _____

6. The bicyclist's mother was out seeing her sister, *who was usually at home.)*
   Meaning: (The bicyclist's mother was usually at home.)

   Revised: _____

7. One brother was home painting the apartment with a friend, *who had a day off from work.*
   Meaning: (The brother had a day off from work.)

   Revised: _____

8. He drove to the hospital, *which was across the street from his home,* in his new car.
   Meaning: (The car was across the street from his home.)

   Revised: _____

9. The brother wanted to talk to the doctor, *whom the bicyclist really respected.*
   Meaning: (The bicyclist really respected his brother.)

   Revised: _____

10. The doctor reassured the brother, *who said the injuries would heal quickly.*
    Meaning: (The doctor said the injuries would heal quickly.)

    Revised: _____

REVIEW EXERCISES

A. Revise the following paragraph by placing each phrase (shown in boldface) as close as possible to the word it describes. Before you move each phrase, think about what meaning makes the most sense. The second sentence has been revised for you. When you have finished, read the revised paragraph to make sure your changes make sense.

She served lots of orders **smelling sweet from the pastry** to friendly customers.

At first, Gloria liked her job in the doughnut shop. She served lots of orders to friendly customers **smelling sweet from the pastry**. She made really good coffee for everyone **made in Brazil**. All the doughnuts were served on painted plates **with jelly fillings**. But then things changed for the worse. The boss told Gloria that she should not serve bowls of soup to customers **filled to the brim**. She also should not stand with customers **talking behind the counter**. Now she works for a boss in a restaurant **with a kind smile and a more relaxed attitude**.

B. Revise the following paragraph by placing each dependent clause (shown in boldface) as close as possible to the word it describes. Before you move the dependent clause, think about which meaning makes the most sense. Add commas when necessary. The second sentence has been revised for you. When you have finished, read the revised paragraph to make sure your changes make sense.

A man **who lived in the building** gave her some useful materials.

Teresa decided to winterize her apartment this year. A man gave her some useful material **who lived in the building**. She nailed the thick plastic material over the windows **that he gave her**. She bought some material in a little shop, **which was made of thick cotton**. Then she made drapes to shut out the cold **that hung to the floor**. She placed weather stripping along the doors, **which came in long, thin strips**. Later she bought small carpets to lay on the cold floor, **which matched the drapes**. The landlord complimented Teresa, **who was inspecting all the apartments**.

C. Revise the following paragraph by placing phrases and dependent clauses as close as possible to the words they describe. Before you move the phrase or dependent clause, think about what meaning makes the most sense. The first sentence has been revised for you. When you have finished, read the revised paragraph to make sure your changes make sense.

Any family **whom you know** might have a fire during the holidays.

Any family might have a fire during the holidays **whom you know**. Holiday fires happen every Christmas and Thanksgiving **which are very dangerous**. Some fires are caused by smokers at parties **with live ashes**. Often during these holidays the weather is cold, and the oil may blow up an apartment or house **that is used as heating fuel**. Christmas gifts and Christmas trees **with wrapping paper all over them** also burn easily. One careless smoker can make a Christmas tree go up in flames **covered with decorations and tinsel**. After Christmas, these trees also can cause serious fires in houses or apartments **drying out their needles indoors**.

_____
_____
_____
_____
_____

Student Assignment

If you have a rough draft of your own that you are revising, look at it now to see if there are any tangled, awkward sentences. If you don't have a rough draft, try writing one. Use the prewriting and drafting instructions in Chapters 1–6. Revise for organization (Chapters 7–12) and sentence structure (Chapters 13–14). Then revise any misplaced phrases and clauses.

Revising Checklist

After you have revised your draft, discuss your writing with your teacher or another person. Use the checklist as a guide.

1. Have I placed each phrase or dependent clause as close as possible to the words it describes?

2. Have I used the correct punctuation for essential and nonessential dependent clauses?

3. Do my revised sentences make my meaning clearer?

4. Do my revised sentences read more smoothly than the ones in the rough draft?

Video Replay

The video shows that when writers discuss their work with another person, the writing improves. When you discuss your writing with another person, how does your writing change? What are your feelings when you work on your writing with another person? How do you feel when you help someone else with his or her writing? Write about these experiences of sharing writing. Then, if you wish, share what you have written with another person.

CHAPTER *16*

REVISING FOR STYLE

Choosing the Right Tone

VIDEO FOCUS

In the video, Tony revises a letter of complaint that Blaine's younger sister has written to her landlord. She has expressed angry feelings in unsuitable language. The tone of her letter may offend the landlord and make the situation worse instead of better. Tony shows Blaine how his sister can express her anger in a businesslike, effective way.

The **tone** of a piece of writing expresses the writer's feelings about the topic and the audience. Choosing the right tone is an important part of the revision process. The right tone is created by using the kind of language that will make your meaning not only clear to your reader but also persuasive. Using the right tone makes the reader feel that you respect his or her way of looking at the topic. It creates the best possible impression for what you have to say.

Chapter Objectives

After seeing the video and completing this chapter, you will understand how to

- use businesslike language
- use everyday language
- use strong language without being offensive.

159

Key Words

Here are some important words that appear in this chapter or on the video. Notice how they are used. If you come across an unfamiliar word that is not on this list, write it down and ask your teacher to explain it to you.

tone
businesslike language, formal language
everyday language

Formal language is sometimes used to describe the same kind of language as **businesslike language**. When we say someone's writing, or way of behaving, is formal, we mean it is done according to strict rules—such as the way a soldier salutes or marches—which may seem stiff and artificial. The kind of businesslike language you should use when you write to someone you do not know well should not be stiff or artificial. It simply should not sound as if you know your reader well, when in fact you do not. In this book, therefore, we use **businesslike language** to describe the writing you will do in your life when handling practical problems with people you do not know well. **Everyday language** and **businesslike language** both are defined more fully in Section 2 of this chapter.

Lesson 1   USING TONE APPROPRIATELY

When you speak, your tone of voice communicates your feelings about the topic and the listener. For example, you can communicate different messages by the various ways (shown in italics) that you say thank you.

"Thank you," she *yelled angrily.*
"Thank you," she *laughed happily.*
"Thank you," she *whispered secretively.*
"Thank you," she *sobbed sadly.*

Whether you speak or write, you communicate your feelings about your topic and your audience through your choice of words. The **tone** of your writing is the result of your choices. For example, if you were writing to a close friend about an act of vandalism, you might write this:

> The cop saw three punks trash the school. Two of the guys
> beat it. The third guy got caught and took the rap.

Calling someone a punk shows that you don't like the way he or she acts. Using words like *cops, punks, guys, trash, beat it,* and *took the rap* shows that you feel close enough to your reader to use everyday language with him or her.

However, if you were the police officer involved in the incident and you were making a formal report to your commanding officer, you might use words such as these:

> I saw three teenagers vandalize the school. Two of the vandals fled. The third teenager was caught and took the blame.

If you as the police officer had used the everyday language of the first example, your commanding officer might have thought you were letting your personal opinion of the teenagers make the report inaccurate. Such a report should give only the facts. A police officer should not communicate his or her opinions or feelings.

However, if you used this impersonal language in a letter to your friend, he or she might wonder why you were using such formal, businesslike words to tell about your experience. Since communicating feelings is an important part of friendship, your friend might think you were hiding your feelings for some reason. Your choice of language would seem strange and leave your friend with questions about your attitude toward him or her.

To decide what tone your writing should have, think about how you feel about your topic and how you want to affect your readers. Use the following checklist to start your thinking.

1. Does your topic make you feel
   worried?
   angry?
   happy?
   proud?
   sad?

2. How do you want your writing to affect your readers? Should it
   get their support?
   stir their anger?
   get them to act?
   make them laugh?
   get them to relax?
   show them that you are on their side?
   scare them?

After you have answered these questions, you are ready to revise your rough draft for tone.

Lesson 2   USING BUSINESSLIKE LANGUAGE

Businesslike language is the kind of language that writers use when they do not know the readers well or when they are writing to governmental or business offices. It is different from **everyday language**, which is used when the readers are close friends or family. Everyday language is what people use in conversation. Writers choose everyday language when they know their readers very well and when the topic is personal.

In the following examples, each sentence shows you a choice of everyday and businesslike language.

	Everyday Language	*Businesslike Language*
Taking inventory is	a snap.	an easy task.
However, Fiona was	bummed out.	upset.
Her supervisor	knocked her work.	criticized her work.
If she blames me, she's	nuts.	mistaken.
I won't take the	rap.	punishment.
I don't	goof off.	waste time.

The choice of words does not affect the meaning of each sentence. It does, however, create two very different tones, which are appropriate for different audiences. Businesslike language is more appropriate in school and at work, whereas everyday language is more appropriate in personal writing and in casual conversation.

Notice that the writer can show feelings using businesslike language. Sometimes it is a good idea to make your feelings known. Just be sure to use language that will not offend your readers and make them unreceptive to your message.

Here are some examples that show different ways of communicating the same meaning, using everyday and businesslike language.

	Everyday Language	*Businesslike Language*
1. Audience:	*a friend*	*newspaper readers*
Topic:	how cooking with Jim bummed me out	how cooking with a friend caused me stress
Jim's salad was	a knockout.	imaginative and delicious.
My spaghetti was a but I	total bomb, kept my cool.	complete failure, stayed calm.

Cooking for ten makes me	burned out.	extremely tired.
Begging for help is	a drag.	depressing.
If help is offered,	that's cool.	it's appreciated.
Being hurried by others	bugs me.	annoys me.

2. Audience:	*former neighbor*	*new job supervisor*
Topic:	how my driving problems are screwing me up	how my transportation problems are making my life difficult
I hope I will	get the hang of driving a car.	feel comfortable with driving a car.
Lack of transportation	drives me crazy.	frustrates me.
My driving teacher was	gross.	very unpleasant.
He said I was	wired.	extremely nervous.
I am in	a jam.	trouble.
My job is	super,	wonderful,
but my driving problems	are a downer.	depress and upset me.

When you choose your tone, be sure to use the words that are most appropriate for your audience and topic.

PRACTICE

Each of the following paragraphs is part of a letter that should be in businesslike language. The words in boldface make the tone of everyday language personal. Revise, making the tone less personal. Substitute appropriate businesslike language for the words in bold-face. The first sentence in each paragraph has been revised for you. When you finish, read the revised paragraph aloud, and listen for the businesslike tone.

1. Job Application Letter

I think I could do a **super** job as a messenger. I am sure I could **get the hang of** the job in a few days. I'll **keep my cool** in an emergency. I will not **goof off** while I am on the job.

Revised

I think I could do a wonderful job as a messenger.

2. Letter to Tenants' Association

I am **ticked off** that it has taken the landlord so long to fix the leaking sink. Having to look at the mess on the kitchen floor is **a real drag**. The constant dripping of the pipes **makes me bananas**. It really **bugs** me that the landlord has not kept his promise to make repairs as soon as they are reported.

Revised

I am angry that it has taken the landlord so long to fix the leaking sink.

3. Consumer Complaint Letter

I am **fed up** with your so-called "easy-to-assemble" doll carriage. The directions say that putting a doll carriage together is **a snap**. For the past four hours, I have been **making myself nuts**, trying to fit the parts in the right places. The reason that I am in **this mess** is that two of the carriage parts are missing. Please send me the two missing pieces so that this doll carriage will not be a **total bomb**.

Revised

*I am upset with your so-called "easy-to-assemble"
doll carriage.*

4. Letter To The City Council

I think putting drunk drivers in **the slammer** is a **super** idea. I do not want to **knock** the cops, who are **swamped** with calls about robberies and other crimes. However, we need a law that says that drunk drivers have to take the **rap** for reckless driving. I know that a night in **the slammer** will **tick off** a lot of drunk drivers, but they need to **shape up**.

Revised

*I think putting drunk drivers in jail is an
excellent idea.*

Student Assignment

If you have a rough draft of your own that you are revising, look at it now to see if the words you have chosen have the right tone for your audience and topic. If you don't have a rough draft, try writing one. Use the prewriting and drafting instructions in Chapters 1–6. Then revise your draft for organization (Chapters 7–12). Revise for sentence structure (Chapters 13–15) and tone.

Revising Checklist

After you have revised your rough draft, discuss your writing with your teacher or another person. Use the checklist as a guide.

1. Did I use the right tone for my audience and topic?

2. If I wrote to a business or governmental office or to someone I do not know well, did I use businesslike language?

3. If I wrote to a close friend or relative, did I use everyday language?

Video Replay

In the video, Tony shows how to express the facts of an upsetting situation in businesslike language. Think of an upsetting situation that you have experienced, such as a problem with a landlord, a store, or an employer. Write about how you handled the situation. Share your writing with another person.

ON YOUR OWN

Eliminating Overuse of *It is* and *There is*

VIDEO FOCUS

In the video, Jolene helps Sharon revise a letter to the housing authority about poor maintenance of the community playground. The power of Sharon's ideas has been weakened by the beginning of several sentences. These sentences begin with **it is** and **there is**, rather than the subject or a word that describes the subject. *It is* and *there is* are empty words. Since they are often used in speaking, they can easily creep into a piece of writing. Writers need to make sure that they do not overuse these words.

Chapter Objectives

After seeing the video and completing this chapter, you will understand how to

- recognize when **It is** or **There is** weakens your writing
- revise sentences beginning with **It is** and **There is**.

Key Words

Here are some important words that appear in this chapter or on the video.

subject   verb

A **subject** is the main topic of a sentence. It is usually a noun. A **noun** is a word that names a person, place, or thing. A person could be *the boy*, or *Mrs. Jones*, or a pronoun like *you, we, I, he*, or *she*. A thing could be *the dog* or *the car* or *the gas company*. A place could be *my house* or *the beach* or *Los Angeles*. A subject can also name an idea (such as *patriotism* or *positive thinking*) or a feeling (such as *love* or *fear*).

A **verb** is a word that describes an action or a feeling, or that enables you to make a statement about a subject. The action it describes can be physical (as in "The boy *runs*," or "The car *hit* the wall"), or mental (as in "We *worry* a lot," or "Mrs. Jones *figured out* her taxes"). A verb of feeling is seen in "The dog *loves* me" or "We *want* more tickets." Verbs are often used also to make statements about subjects, to describe the subjects, as in "The house *is* old," or "We *were* excited."

RECOGNIZING WHEN *IT IS* OR *THERE IS* WEAKENS YOUR WRITING

It is hard answering everyone's questions at once.
There is something I want to tell you.

Notice that the two sentences above can be rewritten without *It is* and *There is*.

Answering everyone's questions at once is hard.
I want to tell you something.

It is and *There is* take up space without giving the reader any information. Most of the time it is better to avoid using them.

Once in a while, however, an idea can be stated more simply and naturally by beginning with a sentence with these words. For example, it is more natural to say

There is enough medical help for the injured.

than it is to say

Enough medical help for the injured **is there**.

Feel free to begin sentences with *It is* and *There is* once or twice in a paragraph. If you use these words more than once or twice, however, they will make your writing vague and boring. If you read your paragraph aloud, you will hear the repetitions that you might miss if you only read silently.

In this chapter, you will find some sentences that begin with *It was*, *There are*, *There were*, or *There was*. Treat them the same way as *It is* and *There is*. Avoid using any of these words too often.

Lesson 1 — REVISING SENTENCES THAT BEGIN WITH *IT IS* AND *THERE IS*

Which of the following sentences gives you more information in the first three words?

> **There are no** rain checks available on these sale items.
> **No rain checks** are available on these sale items.

If you chose the second sentence, you were correct. *There are no* tells you nothing. In the second sentence, *There are* has been eliminated.

You can eliminate empty words from the beginning of a sentence by starting with the subject. In a sentence beginning with *It is* or *There are* and similar empty words, the subject comes after the verb (*rain checks*, the subject, comes after *are*, the verb.) In the revised sentence, the subject is moved to the beginning of the sentence, in front of the verb.

Notice how each of the following sentences is revised by eliminating the empty words and by moving the subject to the beginning of the sentence. The subject of the sentence is shown in boldface.

> **Original:** It is a great experience **to help children learn**.
> **Revised:** **To help children learn** is a great experience.

> **Original:** There is **money** set aside for this purpose.
> **Revised:** **Money** is set aside for this purpose.

> **Original:** It was hard work **moving the piano**.
> **Revised:** **Moving the piano** was hard work.

Sometimes when you eliminate words and move the subject to the beginning of the sentence, you may also need to eliminate words such as *who* or *that*, as shown in the following examples.

> There were **several friends** who helped.
> **Several friends** helped.

> There are **several pianos** that need tuning.
> **Several pianos** need tuning.

Sometimes you may find the subject between two words that make up the verb. In that case, bring the two words of the verb together after the subject. (The two words of the verb are underlined with two lines in each sentence, the subject with one line.)

There <u><u>are</u></u> <u>two piano tuners</u> <u><u>listed</u></u> in the Yellow Pages.
<u>Two piano tuners</u> <u><u>are listed</u></u> in the Yellow Pages.

As you revise your writing, look for sentences that begin with *It is (was)* and *There is (are, was, were)*. Cross out *It (There)* and see how you can rearrange the words that are left. If you find that too many of your revised sentences begin with the subject, look at Chapter 14 to see other ways to begin your sentences.

PRACTICE

A. In each of the following sentences, identify the subject. Then revise the sentence so that *There is (are)* is eliminated. You may also need to eliminate words such as *who* and *that*. Begin your revised sentence with the subject. Read the revised sentence aloud and make sure it makes sense. The first sentence has been done for you.

1. There are two things done with thermostats to save energy.

    Subject: *two things*

    Revised: *Two things are done with thermostats to save energy.*

2. There are some people who check the thermostat with a thermometer.
    Subject: _____

    Revised: _____

3. There is a clocklike thermostat that can adjust the temperature.

    Subject: _____

    Revised: _____

4. There are manuals that give energy-saving ideas to home-owners.

   Subject: _____

   Revised: _____

B. The following paragraphs contain sentences that begin with *It is (was)* and *There is (are, was, were)*. Read each paragraph aloud. Then revise each sentence that begins with these words. Cross out the empty words and rearrange the ones that are left. After you have finished, read the revised paragraphs aloud to hear the differences in rhythm and to make sure your changes make sense. The first sentence has been done for you.

1. It is easy reading a map of the state. There are keys or symbols that indicate major highways. There are numbers that tell the mileage between towns. There are the names of the capital, major cities, and small towns placed on the state map. There is information given on interesting places to visit.

Revised

Reading a map of the state is easy.

_____

_____

_____

2. It was easy filling out the job application form. There was a section called Personal Data that asked the applicant's name and address. There was one section that asked about related job experience. There were several lines provided to describe health problems. There was a space left for applicants to list references.

Revised

_____

_____

3. It is hard work cleaning hotel rooms. There are many rooms that have to be vacuumed and dusted each day. There are sheets and towels that have to be washed, dried, and folded. There are bathroom sinks, tubs, and toilets that need a thorough cleaning. There are dirty dishes from room service that must be returned to the kitchen. There are supervisors who sometimes ask you to redo a poor job.

Revised

_____

_____

_____

_____

Student Assignment

If you have a rough draft that you are revising, look at it now to see if you can eliminate empty words. If you don't have a rough draft, try writing one. Use the prewriting and drafting instructions in Chapters 1–6. Then revise for organization (Chapters 7–12), sentence structure (Chapters 13–15), and tone (Chapter 16). If necessary, eliminate empty words.

Revising Checklist

After you have revised your rough draft to eliminate overuse of empty words, discuss your writing with your teacher or another person. Use the following checklist as a guide.

1. Did I identify sentences that begin with **It is (was)** or **There is (are, was, were)?**

2. Did I revise some of these sentences so that the subject came first?

3. Did I eliminate **who** and **that** also if necessary?

4. Did I bring together the two parts of the verb separated by the subject when I moved the subject to the beginning of the sentence?

5. Are my sentences more interesting now that I have eliminated overuse of these empty words?

Video Replay

In the video, Sharon writes to the Housing Authority Directors about problems with the playground. Have you ever had to write someone in authority about the welfare of your children—an agency, a school principal, a judge, a nurse, or a doctor? Write about your experience. Share your writing with another person.

ON YOUR OWN

CHAPTER *18*

Replacing Dull Words with Vivid Words

VIDEO FOCUS

In the video, Jerry helps Connie revise a letter to her grandmother describing a used car they just bought. Connie has used the word *nice* to describe the car, the weather, the salesman, and the way she and Jerry felt when they chose a car they liked. Jerry shows Connie how to make their experience of buying a car come alive for her grandmother by replacing *nice* with **vivid words**.

Vivid words get the reader's attention because they show a picture that is clear, bright, and alive. They give a sharper picture than **dull, vague words** used to describe the same thing. Vivid words are like a camera that is in focus—they give sharp, colorful images of people, places, or things. Dull, vague words are like a badly focussed camera—they give images that are unclear and boring.

Whether you are using everyday language in a letter to a friend or businesslike language in a letter or in a report to someone in authority, your writing will make a stronger positive impression if the style is vivid.

Chapter Objectives

After seeing the video and completing this chapter, you will understand how to

- identify dull, overused words
- brainstorm for vivid words to replace dull, vague words.

Key Words

Here are some important words that appear in this chapter or on the video.

| dull, vague words | adjectives |
| vivid words | verbs |

When something is **vivid**, it is bright, clear, and alive. Vivid contrasts with **vague**, which means general and unclear, and **dull**, which of course means boring. **Adjectives** are words used to describe persons, places, and things. They answer the questions, which one?, what kind?, and how many? A **verb** is a word that describes an action, a feeling, or allows you to make a statement about the topic of a sentence. (A fuller explanation of verbs is given at the beginning of Chapter 17).

Lesson 1 IDENTIFYING DULL, VAGUE WORDS

This apple is **good**.

This sentence tells the reader about the writer's experience of the apple. From the sentence the reader knows that the writer likes the apple. But is the apple sweet? Is it crunchy or soft? How does it look, taste, smell, or feel? The reader has no way of knowing.

Good, the word the writer used, is dull and vague. Dull, vague words take up space in a sentence without adding specific information. At best, they give the reader a general idea of what is being described. In the foregoing sentence, only the writer knows how the apple tasted. **Good** does not give the reader the specific information needed to create a clear picture of what the writer experienced.

This apple is **sweet**.

Now the reader can imagine the taste of the apple. **Sweet** gives the reader specific information. Vivid words help the reader clearly understand what the writer means. Through their selection of words, writers create pictures. They use words that let the reader see, hear, taste, smell, or feel what the writer is describing.

When writers use a variety of vivid words, they help the reader imagine the person, place, object, or idea they are writing about. In each of the next three sentences, the dull, vague word is in boldface. The vivid words that might replace it is shown in italics.

The movie was **interesting** (*suspenseful*).

That chicken noodle soup smells **funny** (*salty*).

The sausage sandwich tasted **good** (*spicy*).

When you replace the dull, vague word with the vivid word, you get a clearer picture of what is being described.

Dull, vague words may appear when the writer is trying to describe a person, place, thing, or idea. Words that describe are called **adjectives**. You have just seen how to replace dull, vague adjectives with vivid ones.

Another kind of word that can be dull and vague is the action word, or **verb**. In the next section, you will see how to replace a dull, vague verb with a vivid one.

Lesson 2   BRAINSTORMING FOR VIVID WORDS

In Chapter 1, you gathered ideas about your writing topic by brainstorming. You can also use brainstorming to find vivid words. For example, the following sentence will create a clearer picture for the reader if the writer replaces the verb *went* with a vivid word.

Joseph **went** out of the room.

To brainstorm for a vivid word to replace **went**, write *went* at the top of a piece of paper. Then list as many words as you can think of to replace it. If you are having trouble thinking of enough vivid words, look up *go*, the present tense of *went*, in a dictionary or thesaurus.

went

ran	shuffled
strolled	walked
skipped	tiptoed

Each vivid word creates a different picture for the reader.

Vivid Word   *Reader's Picture*

Joseph **ran** out of the room.   Joseph left quickly or suddenly.

Joseph **strolled** out of the room.   Joseph left casually.

Joseph **skipped** out of the room.   Joseph left excitedly or happily, making small jumps.

Joseph **shuffled** out of the room.	Joseph left very slowly, dragging his feet.
Joseph **walked** out of the room.	Joseph left in a normal way, neither fast nor slow.
Joseph **tiptoed** out of the room.	Joseph left very quietly, on tiptoe.

Each of these sentences uses a more vivid word than **went**. The writer must decide which vivid word best communicates the meaning he or she intended. That word should replace **went** in the revised sentence.

Sometimes the writer can choose among several vivid words, depending on what the word is describing and the intended meaning of the sentence. For example, in Section 1 of this chapter, the writer has brainstormed three vivid words for each use of the word *good*. The final choice in each case depends on what *good* is describing and the intended meaning of the sentence.

Dull Word	*Brainstormed Vivid Words*
Today was a **good** day.	relaxing, sunny, productive
I was offered a **good** job.	well-paying, rewarding, easy
I wore a **good** suit to the interview.	expensive, well-made, new
Afterward, I had a **good** dinner with a **good** friend.	delicious, nutritious, filling loyal, thoughtful, long-time

When you select a vivid word to replace a dull, vague one, be sure that the new word clearly and accurately communicates your intended meaning.

PRACTICE

A. In the following list, each *dull word* (in boldface) is used in a sentence. Brainstorm three *vivid words* that could replace each dull word. Be sure the vivid words do not change your intended meaning. Write the brainstormed words in the spaces next to the word they replace. The first example has been done for you.

1. The movie was **bad**.   *gory*   *boring*   *silly*
2. A **beautiful** cat sat in the window.   _____   _____   _____
3. The **big** house is for sale.   _____   _____   _____

4. The crowd **came** through the _____ _____ _____
door.

5. Taking drugs is **dumb**. _____ _____ _____

6. We received an **exciting** _____ _____ _____
present.

7. You did a **fine** job. _____ _____ _____

8. We sang **fun** songs. _____ _____ _____

9. We bought a **good** engine for _____ _____ _____
our car.

10. My sister wore a **great** _____ _____ _____
outfit.

11. The weather is **terrific**. _____ _____ _____

12. My new coworker is a **neat** _____ _____ _____
person.

13. I am lucky to have a **nice** _____ _____ _____
boss.

14. My friend grows **pretty** _____ _____ _____
flowers.

15. The boy **hurt** his hand. _____ _____ _____

16. The weather on vacation was _____ _____ _____
wonderful.

17. "I'm stronger than you," she _____ _____ _____
said.

18. He **moved** his hand from the _____ _____ _____
fire.

19. The auto accident was _____ _____ _____
awful.

20. The dog **touched** his hand. _____ _____ _____

B. For each sentence in Exercise A you brainstormed three vivid words. Choose two words from each group of three and use them in two new sentences of your own. Draw on your own experience, or what you know from other people, movies, books, magazines, or television. The sentences do not have to be long. The first example has been done for you.

1. *The fight was gory. My last vacation was boring.*

2. _____

3. _____

4. _____

5. _____

6. _____

7. _____

8. _____

9. _____

10. _____

11. _____

12. _____

13. _____

14. _____

15. _____

16. _____

17. _____

18. _____

19. _____

20. _____

C. Revise the following paragraph by replacing the dull, vague words (in bold italics) with vivid words. For each dull word, brainstorm at least three vivid words. Write them in the spaces provided. You may wish to use one of the words you listed in Exercise A. Then, circle the best vivid word for each sentence and revise the paragraph. The first sentence has been done for you. Make sure the new word makes sense in the sentence and in the paragraph.

Yesterday was a ***good*** (*productive*, happy, **exciting**) day for Jim. He ***got*** (_____, _____, _____) out of bed very early so he would have the whole day free. He ***went*** (_____, _____, _____) to the department store as fast as he could to buy work clothes that were on sale. While he was shopping, he found a ***nice*** (_____, _____, _____) pair of jeans. Later he bought some ***neat*** (_____, _____, _____) boots. On the way home, he stopped at a small sporting goods store and bought a ***wonderful*** (_____, _____, _____) backpack.

Revised

Yesterday was a productive day for Jim.

_____

_____

_____

D. Revise the following paragraph by replacing each dull, vague word with a vivid word. First, identify the dull words. Then, brainstorm at least three vivid words for each dull word. Select the best vivid word and revise the sentence. After you have revised the paragraph, reread it to make sure it makes sense.

> The month I spent in the Alcoholism Rehabilitation Center was great. The counselors were good. I thought about the dumb reasons I drank. Giving up drinking was bad, but they told me that continuing to drink would be worse.

Revised

_____

_____

_____

_____

REVIEW EXERCISE

Revise the following paragraph by replacing the dull, vague words with vivid words. There are more verbs among the dull, vague words in this paragraph than in the earlier exercises. Often, you can improve the style of your writing by using more specific, active verbs to describe an event or series of events. The dull, vague words are in boldface. Brainstorm for vivid words and choose the best ones. Do not use the same vivid word twice.

> The storm last week was **terrible**. Water **ran** down the streets of our town. It **came** through the windows of our house. A tree even **came** through our roof. Next door,

the wind **took** the roof off our neighbor's house. Garbage cans **went** down the street. I saw my little brother outside on the porch. I **said** to him, "Get down here in the cellar!" He **came** right through the cellar window. The flood water **wet** a lot of our furniture. We certainly felt **better** when the storm was finally over the next morning.

Student Assignment

If you have a rough draft of your own that you are revising, look at it now to see if it contains any dull, vague words. If you don't have a rough draft, try writing one. Use the prewriting and drafting instructions in Chapters 1–6. Revise for organization (Chapters 7–12), sentence structure (chapters 13–15), and tone (Chapter 16). Eliminate overuse of empty words such as **It is** and **There is** (Chapter 17). Finally, replace, dull, vague words with vivid ones.

Revising Checklist

After you have revised your rough draft, discuss your writing with you teacher or another person. Use the checklist as a guide.

1. Did I identify the dull, vague words in my writing?
2. Did I brainstorm for vivid words to replace the dull words?
3. Did I vary my choice of words so that the same words did not appear over and over again?
4. Did the vivid words I chose clearly and accurately communicate my intended meaning?

Video Replay

In the video, Connie wanted to make her words vivid enough to excite her shut-in grandmother. Think of an exciting event in your life. Describe it in a letter to a relative or friend. Make sure your words are vivid. Share your writing with another person.

UNIT 4

EDITING AND SHARING

PREPARING YOUR FINAL REVISION FOR YOUR READERS, AND SHARING IT WITH THEM

You have reached the last stage of the writing process.

After all your revisions for organization and for style are finished, you must look over your writing to make sure it is completely correct in grammar, and in mechanics (**punctuation, capitalization**, and **spelling**). This part of the writing process is called **editing**. The chapters in this unit take you through the basic steps of checking a piece of writing for correctness.

1. Checking for correct sentence structure: Have I written every idea as a complete thought in a correct sentence?

2. Checking for correct usage (use of subjects, verbs, and pronouns): Are all the verbs in the correct tense? Do all the subjects agree with their verbs? Are all the pronouns used correctly and clearly?

3. Checking for correct mechanics (punctuation, capitalization, spelling): Are all the words spelled correctly? Are all the words and sentences punctuated correctly? Are all the appropriate words capitalized correctly?

This last stage of the writing process may not be the most exciting, but it is necessary if your writing is going to make the best possible impression on your readers. It also expresses pride in your work to check it carefully. If you make sure your work is free of mistakes, you will feel better about sharing it. You will want others to read it. You may even want to get it published, either by writing a letter to a newspaper or by putting it in a newsletter. If you become really interested in writing and find yourself writing a lot, you might even want to have some of your work printed by one of the inexpensive kinds of computer printers now available.

CHAPTER *19* *EDITING*

Checking for Run-on Sentences and Fragments

VIDEO FOCUS

In the video, Angela helps Jolene edit a letter to a medical clinic. Jolene would like the clinic to mail her daughter's immunization records to her new school. The letter contains two complete thoughts that are run together because they are not correctly punctuated and capitalized.

In order to write clearly and correctly, you always must express complete thoughts in sentences. Neither **run-on sentences** nor **fragments** are sentences. Fragments are groups of words that do not express complete thoughts. Run-on sentences run complete thoughts together incorrectly. Both must be changed into sentences that make your writing clear and correct.

Run-on sentences and fragments are very serious writing mistakes. They make a bad impression on readers and are often confusing. Learning to correct them is essential for writing that will be understood and respected.

Chapter Objectives

After seeing the video and completing the chapter, you will understand how to

- identify run-on sentences and fragments
- edit for correct punctuation and capitalization.

Key Words

Here are some important words that appear in this chapter or on the video. If you come across a word that is not on this list, write it down and ask your teacher to explain it to you.

run-on sentence   punctuation
fragment   capitalization

Lesson 1   SEPARATING RUN-ON SENTENCES INTO SENTENCES

In the video, Jolene corrects two run-on sentences in her letter in two ways. She has a friend read her writing aloud so she can hear where her voice drops. The drop in her voice indicates the end of a complete thought. Jolene also reads all her sentences backwards to help herself separate the complete thoughts more clearly.

Run-on sentences often make a reader unsure of the writer's meaning, because he or she cannot tell where one complete thought ends and the next one begins. To correct run-on sentences, you must separate the complete thoughts clearly and punctuate them properly. Read the following examples of run-on sentences.

1. Hector and Consuela discussed sharing the care for their elderly parents they decided to take turns doing the shopping, cooking, and cleaning.

2. Why were their parents so concerned about keeping their independence they needed the help.

3. Hector and Consuela were amazed they hadn't realized how their parents felt.

Each example looks like a very long sentence, because it begins with a capital letter and ends with a period. However, each one is really two sentences, because it expresses more than one complete thought.

When you talk, you separate your thoughts by pausing or taking a breath. When you write, you need to separate your thoughts by showing these pauses in your writing. To do this, you must use correct **punctuation** (a period, a question mark, or an exclamation point at the end of every sentence) and correct **capitalization** (a capitalized letter on the first letter of the first word in every sentence). A run-on sentence runs two complete thoughts together without correct punctuation and capitalization. To correct it, you must separate the two thoughts clearly into two sentences using proper punctuation and capitalization.

Here are the run-on sentences you just read. Each one has been separated by adding the correct punctuation and capitalization.

1. Hector and Consuela discussed sharing the care for their elderly parents. They decided to take turns doing the shopping, cooking, and cleaning.

2. Why were their parents so concerned about keeping their independence? They needed the help.

3. Hector and Consuela were amazed! They hadn't realized how their parents felt.

Notice how the writer's message is clearer now that the sentences contain correct punctuation and capitalization.

PRACTICE

Edit the following paragraphs by adding the correct punctuation and capitalization to the run-ons. The first run-on sentence has been corrected for you. After you have finished each paragraph, reread it to make sure your changes make sense.

Next Friday our work shift is having a farewell party for Henrietta she is moving to another city. Everyone is invited to attend the party, it will be held at Michelle' home. We would like each person to bring a snack the party will begin at 7:00 P.M. We hope that everyone will attend, let's celebrate.

Edited

Next Friday our work shift is having a farewell
party for Henrietta. She is moving to another city.

_____

_____

_____

To obtain your driver's license, you must pass a written test and a road test the Motor Vehicle Bureau wants to make sure that drivers know the rules of the road. What kind of questions can you expect the written test asks you about road signs, speed limits, and safety rules, watching the signs and talking to expert drivers will help you prepare you should also study the manual.

Edited

_____

_____

_____

_____

_____

_____

You also can change run-on sentences into correct sentences by connecting, instead of separating, the two complete thoughts. You already have learned how to do this in *Chapter 13: Varying Sentence Lengths*. In that chapter you learned about three different kinds of connecting words to use in combining short sentences into one longer sentence. You should keep those connector words in mind when you are editing. You might want to use them in correcting run-on sentences also.

Lesson 2   MAKING FRAGMENTS INTO SENTENCES

Read the following examples. After you read them, ask yourself if they sound complete in their meaning.

Before you buy a box of cereal.
Reading the label on a cereal box.
If sugar is listed in the first five ingredients.
Cereals an important source of fiber.
Cereals with high fiber and low sugar content.
Which makes me angry.
Coffee that is on the shelf.
The manager who runs the store.
Who piled boxes on the floor.
Waking up to go to work.
The waiter who is learning his job.
If I exercise regularly.
When I eat fruit for breakfast.

After reading these groups of words, you probably felt or heard that something was wrong. They all give a feeling of incompleteness. Since they all begin with a capital letter and end with a period, they look like sentences. They are not sentences, however, because they do not express complete thoughts. Words need to be added to make the meaning of each statement complete.

A **fragment** is a group of words that (a) does not express a complete thought, (b) begins with a capital letter, and (c) ends with a period. Although we often speak in fragments, we should not use them when we write. Here is how each of the fragments in the list at the beginning of this lesson might be changed into a complete sentence. Notice that some fragments can be changed into sentences in several ways. How you change a fragment into a sentence depends on what you want to say, or the way you want to say it.

Adding words to the fragment

Before you buy a box of cereal, you should read the label.

Reading the label on a cereal box gives you information about ingredients.

If sugar is listed in the first five ingredients, the cereal contains a lot of it.

Cereals can be **an important source of fiber**.

Cereals with high fiber and low sugar content are the healthiest.

Coffee is one item **that is on the shelf**.

Mr. Hertz is **the manager who runs the store**.

He is the clerk **who piled boxes on the floor**.

Her smoking, **which makes my angry**, is unhealthy.

Taking away words from the fragment

~~Before you~~ Buy a box of cereal.
~~If~~ Sugar is listed in the first five ingredients.
Coffee ~~that~~ is on the shelf.
The manager ~~who~~ runs the store.
The waiter ~~who is~~ learning his job.
~~When~~ I eat fruit for breakfast.

Taking away words and adding words to the fragment

Some cereals ~~with~~ high fiber and low sugar content.

~~Before~~ You might buy a box of cereal sometime.

Combining the fragment with a complete thought that comes just before or just after it

1. My day starts right. **When I eat fruit for breakfast.**

Combined:

My day starts right when I eat fruit for breakfast.

2. **Waking up to go to work.** I turn off the alarm.

Combined:

Waking up to go to work, I turn off the alarm.

3. I feel stronger and more relaxed. **If I exercise regularly.**

Combined:

I feel stronger and more relaxed if I exercise regularly.

4. **The waiter who is learning his job.** He has a hard time on the first day of work.

Combined:

The waiter who is learning his job has a hard time on the first day.

Notice that when you combine fragments with sentences, you sometimes take away one word or more.

All the ways of correcting fragments shown above give complete meaning to these groups of words that do not express complete thoughts. Fragments like those above are either phrases or dependent clauses. *Phrases* (as you learned in Chapter 14) are groups of words that do not have a subject or a verb, or both. *Dependent clauses* (as you learned in Chapter 15) are groups of words which have a subject and a verb but do not express a complete thought. By changing these groups of words into statements that express complete thoughts, you make fragments into sentences.

A. Find each fragment in the following paragraph and make it into a sentence by combining it with a sentence that comes before or after it. Remember that when you combine fragments in order to make sentences, you sometimes may add or take away words or do both. The first fragment has been corrected for you.

> The laundry workers who clean all types of clothes. They have many duties. They replace lost buttons and mend seams. Before they wash the clothes. They break down grease spots. Using stain removers. The spots which disappear. During the washing. After the clothes are washed. They are packaged. The workers that package them. Doing all the work by hand.

Edited

The laundry workers who clean all types of clothes also do minor repairs.

B. Make each fragment into a complete sentence by adding or taking away words, or by both adding and taking them away. The first fragment has been completed for you. After you have finished, reread the sentences to make sure they make sense.

> The waiter who is learning his job. Some customers with big appetites and short tempers. Can't make up their minds what to order. After the waiter writes the customers' order on the ticket. It taken to the kitchen. The cook who runs the kitchen. It full of waiters. Yelling and running around. If they try to be polite and give quick service. The customers are satisfied.

Edited

The waiter is learning his job.

Lesson 3 FINDING FRAGMENTS AND RUN-ON SENTENCES IN A PARAGRAPH

Sometimes it is difficult to identify fragments and run-on sentences in your own writing. When you read your own writing, you often do not notice when you have used fragments and run-on sentences. Your mind supplies the missing parts, and proper punctuation.

A good way to find fragments and run-on sentences is to read the paragraph backwards, sentence by sentence. Use this procedure:

1. Number your sentences.

2. Go to the end of the paragraph and find the last sentence.

3. Read it.

4. Ask yourself: Is it a correct sentence or is it a fragment or a run-on sentence? If it is a fragment, make it into a sentence by adding or taking away words, or doing both. You can also combine the fragment with a sentence before or after it. If it is a run-on sentence, separate it into sentences by adding a period, a question mark, or an exclammation point at the end of the first complete thought. Then capitalize the first word of the second complete thought.

5. Go backwards to the next sentence. Read it and repeat step 4.

6. Continue the procedure until you have read and checked all the sentences in the paragraph.

7. After you have worked your way backwards through the paragraph, sentence by sentence, read the paragraph forward in the normal manner. If you have made any changes, be sure that all of the sentences are correct and that they make sense.

Here is an example of how this procedure works.

1. Saving money on long-distance calls. 2. By knowing how and when to call. 3. The telephone directory contains information on the best times to make calls, it tells you when the lowest and highest rates are. 4. Dialing long-distance number direct costs less than calling the operator for assistance it also takes less time. 5. If you check with your telephone company. 6. You may find that it has a special calling plan to reduce long-distance phone bills.

Go to the last sentence.

6. You may find that it has a special calling plan to reduce long-distance phone bills.

Is it a sentence, a fragment, or a run-on sentence? **It is a sentence.**

If it is a sentence, go backwards to the next sentence.

5. If you check with your telephone company.

Is it a sentence, a fragment, or a run-on sentence? **It is a fragment.**

If it is a fragment, make it into a sentence. If it is a run-on sentence, make it into two complete sentences, or connect the two complete thoughts correctly.

> If you check with your telephone company, you may find it has a special calling plan that can reduce long-distance phone bills.

Go backwards to the next sentence.

4. Dialing the long-distance number direct costs less than calling the operator for assistance it also takes less time.

Is it a sentence, a fragment, or a run-on sentence? **It is a run-on sentence.**

If it is a fragment, make it into a sentence. If it is a run-on sentence, make it into two complete sentences, or connect the two complete thoughts correctly.

> Dialing the long-distance number direct costs less than calling the operator for assistance. It also takes less time.

Go backwards to the next sentence.

3. The telephone directory contains information on the best times to make calls, it tells you when the lowest and highest rates are.

Is it a sentence, a fragment, or a run-on sentence? **It is a run-on sentence.**

If it is a fragment, make it into a sentence. If it is a run-on sentence, make it into two complete sentences, or connect the two complete thoughts correctly.

> The telephone directory contains information on the best times to make calls. It tells you when the lowest and highest rates are.

Go backwards to the next sentence.

2. By knowing how and when to call.

Is it a sentence, a fragment, or a run-on sentence? **It is a fragment.**

If it is a fragment, make it into a sentence. If it is a run-on sentence, make it into two complete sentences, or connect the two complete thoughts correctly.

You can save money by knowing how and when to call.

Go backwards to the next sentence.

1. Saving money on long-distance calls.

Is it a sentence, a fragment, or a run-on sentence? **It is a fragment.**

If it is a fragment, make it into a sentence. If it is a run-on sentence, make it into two complete sentences, or connect the two complete thoughts correctly.

Saving money on long-distance calls is easy.

Now read the entire paragraph forwards in the normal way. Check to be sure that all the sentences are really sentences and that the paragraph makes sense.

Here is the edited paragraph.

Saving money on long-distance calls is easy. You can save money by knowing how and when to call. The telephone directory contains information on the best times to make calls. It tells you when the lowest and highest rates are. Dialing the number direct costs less than calling the operator for assistance. It also takes less time. If you check with your telephone company, you may find it has a calling plan that can reduce long-distance phone bills.

Review Exercises

A. Edit the following paragraphs by making the fragments and run-on sentences into complete sentences. Use the procedure outlined above. The first correction has been done for you. After you have finished, reread the paragraph forwards to make sure that all the sentences are really sentences and that the paragraph makes sense.

1. I am writing to complain about the sweater which I bought from your catalog the sweater was not made properly. **2.** Because the sweater seams are uneven. **3.** Also, one sleeve three inches longer than the other. **4.** The bottom hem is uneven. **5.** The back being shorter than the front. **6.** I am returning the sweater I want a full refund.

Corrections

6. I am returning the sweater. I want a full refund.

5. _____

4. _____

3. _____

2. _____

1. _____

Edited

I am writing to complain about the sweater which I bought from your catalog.

_____

_____

_____

1. Most job application forms which ask for similar information. **2.** The forms ask for personal information personal information includes your full name, mailing address, phone number, Social Security number, and date of birth. **3.** The forms with questions about your education and your work experience. **4.** Depending on the type of job. **5.** Some employers want you to list medical information about illnesses. **6.** Take all this information with you it will help you fill out the application form.

Corrections

6. _____

5. _____

4. _____

3. _____

2. _____

1. _____

Edited

_____

_____

_____

_____

_____

Student Assignment

If you have a rough draft that is ready for editing, look now to see if it contains any fragments or run-on sentences. If you don't have a rough draft, try writing one. Use the prewriting and drafting instructions in Chapters 1–6. Then revise for organization (see Chapters 7–12) and style (Chapters 13–18). Finally, make all fragments and run-on sentences into sentences.

Editing Checklist

After you have edited your rough draft, show it to your teacher or another person. Use the checklist as a guide.

1. Did I find fragments and run-on sentences by reading my paragraph backwards sentence by sentence?

2. Did I make each fragment into a sentence by adding or taking away words, by doing both, or by combining the fragment with a complete thought?

3. Did I separate run-on sentences into two or more sentences by adding correct punctuation and capitalization?

4. Did I reread my paragraph forwards to make sure that all the sentences were really sentences and the paragraph make sense?

Video Replay

In the video, Jolene has recently moved. It is important to have her daughter's immunization records transferred to her new school. What are some of the things you need to do when you move? Write your thoughts and share your writing with another person.

ON YOUR OWN

20 *EDITING*

Checking for Verb Tenses and Subject–Verb Agreement

VIDEO FOCUS

In the video, Sharon edits a letter to her district election office. She would like the office to send voter registration forms to her new address. The letter contains verbs that are incorrect because they are in the wrong tense for the different actions her letter refers to.

Writers use the *tense of a verb* to tell the *time of the action*—the past, the present, or the future. If a writer uses the wrong verb tense for an action, the reader will be confused about the time of the action. To avoid this confusion, use of verb tense must be consistent. Something is consistent when it always happens in the same way. **Consistent verb tense** means that the same tense always is used with the same time of the action: **present** or **present continuous tense** with present time; **past tense** with past time; **future tense** with future time. Consistent verb tenses enable the reader to understand clearly *when* the action is happening.

Subject-Verb Agreement is also essential for writing that is going to be respected. The basic rule of subject-verb agreement is: singular subjects always take singular verbs, and plural subjects always take plural verbs. Problems of agreement are especially common with (1) **sentences with two or more subjects,** and (2) **the third person singular**, which includes subjects that can be replaced by the pronouns, *he, she,* and *it.* You will do many exercises with subject-verb agreement, as well as with verb tense, in this chapter.

Chapter Objectives

After seeing the video and completing this chapter, you will understand how to

- edit for correct verb tenses
- edit for subject–verb agreement.

Key Words

Here are some important words that appear in this chapter or on the video. If you come across a word that is not on this list, write it down and ask your teacher to explain it to you.

present tense

present continuous tense

past tense

future tense

consistent verb tense, consistency of tenses

subject–verb agreement

singular

plural

the third person singular

Lesson 1 IDENTIFYING THE VERB TENSE

In her letter in the video, Sharon uses three different verb tenses because she is writing about things that happen at three different times—the present, the past, and the future. Often, however, you will write about actions that happen only at one time. If you know your verb tenses, you will be able to write correctly in the same tense for events that happen at the same time.

Read the following pairs of sentences. Decide whether the time of the action is the past, the present, or the future. (The verb, or action word, is in boldface.)

Geraldo **is cleaning** the carpets **now**.
Each morning I **arrive** at work, and I **check** the work assignment chart.

The action in the first sentence above is happening right now, so the verb is in the **present continuous tense**. The two actions in the second sentence happen on a regular basis, so the verbs are in the **present tense**. Read the following pairs of sentences.

Geraldo **cleaned** the carpets **last night**.
I **arrived** at work **yesterday**, and I **checked** the work assignment chart.

The actions in the two preceding sentences happened in the past and were completed in the past, so the verbs are in the **past tense**. Read the following pairs of sentences.

> **Next week**, Geraldo **will clean** the carpets.
> **Tomorrow morning** I will arrive at work, and I **will check** the work assignment chart.

The actions in the two preceding sentences will happen later, so the verbs are in the **future tense**.

Lesson 2 MAKING SURE THE VERB TENSES ARE CONSISTENT

You must keep all your verbs in one tense if you are writing about one time. If you change the verb tense you are using, it must be clear why you are changing from one time to another time or you will confuse your reader. Read the following paragraph for an example of confusing tense changes.

> I **work** at a new job as a bus mechanic. It **was** exciting to receive a regular paycheck. My supervisor **is teaching** me how to repair the engine of a bus. I **liked** the work, and **will improve** my skills.

Has the job ended, is it going on now, or will it start in the future? It's impossible to tell, because the tenses keep changing back and forth between past, present, and future.

If the job in the example is in the present, the verbs should be in the present tense and the present continuous tense.

> I **am working** (*present continuous tense*) at a new job as a bus mechanic this week. It **is** (*present tense*) exciting to receive a regular paycheck. My supervisor **is teaching** (*present continuous tense*) me how to repair the engine of a bus. I **like** (*present tense*) the work a lot, and **am improving** (*present continuous tense*) my skills.

If the job is an action that happened in the past and was completed in the past, the verbs should be in the past tense.

> I **worked** at a new job as a bus mechanic last week. It **was** exciting to receive a regular paycheck. My supervisor **taught** me how to repair the engine of a bus. I **liked** the work a lot, and **improved** my skills.

If the job in the example begins in the future, the verbs should be in the future tense, as follows.

> I **will work** at a new job as a bus mechanic next week. It **will be** exciting to receive a regular paycheck. My supervisor **will teach** me how to repair the engine of a bus. I **will like** the work, and **will improve** my skills.

Sometimes, however, like Sharon in the video, you need to use several different tenses in the same paragraph because you are writing about a subject in which different things happen at different times. Here is the same paragraph about the new job rewritten so that one part of the action is going on right now, two parts of it happen on a regular basis, one happened in the past, and one will happen later.

> I **am working** (*present continuous tense*) at a new job as a bus mechanic now. It **is** (*present tense*) exciting to receive a regular paycheck. My supervisor **taught** (*past tense*) me how to repair the engine of a bus. I **like** my work a lot (*present time*), and **will improve** (*future tense*) my skills.

To check for correct use of verb tenses in a paragraph, first ask yourself when each event described in each sentence occurred. Is it happening right now (present continuous tense)? Or does it happen on a regular basis (present tense)? Has it already happened and been completed (past tense)? Will it happen later (future tense)?

After you have decided on the correct verb tense for each sentence, read the entire paragraph. Be sure that the verb tenses are correct for the time when each action occurs. As a general rule, avoid mixing verb tenses in a single sentence. In a paragraph, change the tenses from one sentence to another only if the different things that happen occur at different times.

PRACTICE

A. Edit the following paragraph so that all verbs (in boldface) are in the present tense. The first sentence has been edited for you. When you are finished, reread the edited paragraph to be sure that your changes make sense.

> On Fridays and Saturdays, Dolores **will work** at the information desk in the shopping center. Every day she **will answer** questions about the stores and restaurants. She **gave** people maps of the shopping center. Dolores also

helped customers find the rest rooms and public telephones. Sometimes she **will help** lost children find their parents. Dolores **will like** her job because she **helped** people.

Edited

On Fridays and Saturdays, Dolores works at the information desk in the shopping center.

B. Now edit the preceding paragraph so that all the verbs are in the past tense. The first sentence has been edited for you.

Edited

On Fridays and Saturdays, Dolores worked at the information desk in the shopping center.

C. The verb tenses in the following paragraph are inconsistent. Identify the verbs. Then chose a time for the action. Edit the paragraph so that the tenses are consistent for that time. When you have finished, reread the edited paragraph to make sure your changes make sense.

The boiler in my building sometimes will break down. Usually, the tenants complained right away. Then, the superintendent is calling the repair service. Later, the service will send someone to fix the boiler. Until the boiler is fixed, the tenants had no heat or hot water. Of course, the people in the building will be very angry about this situation.

Edited

Lesson 3 AGREEMENT OF SUBJECT AND VERB IN THE PRESENT TENSE

Agreement of subjects and verbs means that singular subjects have singular verbs and plural subjects have plural verbs. It may help you to make subjects and verbs agree if you remember these basic facts about verbs and their subjects:

Singular and Plural Verb Forms in the Present Tense

In the present tense, the only form in regular verbs that is different is **the third person singular**, which refers to subjects that can be replaced by **he, she,** or **it**. The third person singular *always* ends in **-s** or **-es**.

Singular (the verb, to pay)	**Plural**
I pay taxes.	We pay taxes.
You pay taxes.	You pay taxes.
He pay**s** taxes.	They pay taxes.
She pay**s** taxes.	
It (the corporation) pay**s** taxes.	

Singular (the verb, to watch)	**Plural**
I watch TV.	We watch TV.
You watch TV.	You watch TV.
He watch**es** TV.	They watch TV.
She watch**es** TV.	
It (the cat) watch**es** the fly.	

Final *-s* or *-es* with Singular and Plural Subjects and Verbs

Generally, plural subjects end in an **-s** or an **-es**; singular subjects do not. As a general rule, when a subject ends in an **-s** or an **-es**, its verb does not; when a subject does not end in an **-s** or an **-es**, its verbs does.

The boy enjoys sports. (singular)	**The boy enjoys sports. (plural)**
The car goes fast. (singular)	The cars go fast. (plural)
The bus arrives late. (singular)	The buses arrive late. (plural)
Her kiss feels nice. (singular)	Her kisses feel nice. (plural)

Agreement with Two Subjects Joined by *and*

Often, when two singular subjects are joined by *and*, a plural subject is created. Two subjects joined by *and* take a plural verb.

Unit 4   Editing and Sharing

George *and* Miss Jones are engaged.

He *and* his wife like Mexican food.

When two or more subjects are joined by these pairs of words—**either/or, neither/nor, not only/but also**—the verb agrees with the closer subject.

If the subject closer to the verb is singular, use a singular verb (a verb ending in **-s** or **-es**, usually).

Either the taxi cabs **or** the bus *needs* a tune-up.

Neither the customers **nor** the manager *likes* the rude clerk.

Not only the boxes **but also** the bottle *is leaking*.

If the subject closer to the verb is plural, use a plural verb form (no **-s** or **-es** ending).

Either the bus **or** the taxi cabs *need* a tune-up.

Neither the manager **nor** the customers *like* the rude clerk.

Not only the bottle **but also** the boxes *are leaking*.

Lesson 4   OTHER PATTERNS OF SUBJECT–VERB AGREEMENT

1. Words that come between the subject and the verb do not affect agreement.

The **bottle** of pills *costs* more than a box of cough drops.

(*Bottle* is the singular subject. *Costs* is the singular verb. Pills is plural but does not affect agreement.)

The **supervisor**, along with the workers, *wants* a new contract.

(*Supervisor* is the singular subject. *Wants* is the singular verb. *Workers* is plural but does not affect agreement.)

The **workers**, as well as the supervisor, *want* a new contract.

(*Workers* is a plural subject. *Want* is the plural verb. *Supervisor* is singular but does not affect agreement.)

Raymond, not Maggie, *washes* the dishes at the cafe.

(*Raymond* is the singular subject. *Washes* is the singular verb. *Raymond* is not joined to Maggie by *and*, so the verbs refers only to *Raymond*.)

2. All of the words in the following list are singular. When they are the subjects of sentences in the present tense, they take the third person singular form of the verb: the verb form that ends in **-s** or **-es**.

everyone	everybody	everything	each
someone	somebody	something	each one
anyone	anybody	anything	either
no one	nobody	nothing	neither

Everybody in the union *likes* the new health plan.
Someone with a low salary *worries* about his or her rent.
Nothing *works* in this place.
Everything the children want *costs* too much.
Each of the employees *receives* a quarterly performance evaluation.
Either of those girls always *wins* the prize.

3. When a sentence begins with the word *there*, the subject follows the verb. The verb must still agree with the subject.

There *are* **thirty applicants** for the same job.

(*Applicants* is the plural subject. *Are* is the plural verb.)

There *is* **a rule** against drinking on the job.

(*Rule* is the singular subject. *Is* is the singular verb.)

There *goes* **the siren**.

(*Siren* is the singular subject. *Goes* is the singular verb.)

There *go* **the sirens**.

(*Sirens* is the plural subject. *Go* is the plural verb.)

PRACTICE

In each of the following paragraphs, the subject (underlined once) and the verb (underlined twice) of each sentence do not agree. Decide whether the subject is singular or plural. Change each verb so that it agrees with the subject of the sentence. Then rewrite the edited paragraph. Preceding each paragraph, you will find one or two hints that tell you what rules of agreement will help you. The first verb has been changed for you.

1. **Hint:** A singular subject takes a singular verb. A plural subject takes a plural verb. A plural subject may be formed by joining two singular subjects with *and*.

> 1. George and Jim *washes* the windows of our building. 2. **My husband and I** *worries* about their safety. 3. **They** *works* on old, weak ladders. 4. **Their window-washer safety belts** *is* also old. 5. **Wet weather and high winds** *make* their job especially dangerous. 6. **These men**, however, *does* good work. 7. **My husband** *tell* them so frequently.

Edited

George and Jim wash the windows in our building.

2. **Hint:** In a sentence that begins with *there*, the subject and verb must still agree. Words between the subject and verb do not affect agreement.

> 1. There *is* many contagious **diseases**. 2. **AIDS**, one of these diseases, *need* certain conditions to spread. 3. The **body fluids** of an infected person *communicates* the virus. 4. Therefore, **sexual activity** with many people *increase* the risk of getting sick. 5. **Drug addicts** who share needles and have sex with different partners *spreads* the virus. 6. Pregnant **women**, who may have the virus, sometimes *infects* their babies. 7. Every year, there *is* many more **victims** of this fatal disease.

Edited

_____

_____

_____

3. **Hint:** Words such as *everyone* and *everything* are treated as one person or thing.

> 1. **Each person** you meet *look* at life in a special way. 2. **Everyone**, however, *have* fantasies about a personal hero. 3. A hero is **somebody** who *do* things you only dream about doing. 4. Because **everything** about that person's life *seem* good to you, that person is your hero. 5. **Anybody** who is a fan of a hero *make* the hero into a god. 6. **Nothing** that the hero does wrong *change* the fan's idea of his or her god.

Edited

_____

_____

_____

_____

_____

4. **Hint:** In a sentence with two subjects joined by *or, nor*, or *but also*, the verb agrees with the subject that is nearer.

> 1. Not only **negative changes** but also **positive changes** in your life *causes* stress. 2. Either **a new job** or **a new relationship** *make* changes in the way you experience things. 3. Not only **divorces** but also **a new marriage** *are* stressful. 4. Sometimes, either **a nervous stomach** or **breathing difficulties** *comes* from such stressful changes. 5. Often neither **pills** nor **sleep** *reduce* the tension much. 6. However, either **physical exercises** or **a hot bath** *relieve* stress symptoms for some people.

Edited

_____

_____

_____

_____

_____

A. The following paragraph contains errors in consistency of verb tenses. Decide which verb tense makes the most sense for the paragraph—past, present, or future. Make all verbs consistent in that tense. Then reread the edited paragraph to make sure that your corrections make sense.

> 1. There were several advantages to using a credit card. 2. Credit cards lets me buy things when I was short of cash. 3. They also will be safer than carrying a lot of cash. 4. At the end of the month, I wrote only one check to pay for all the charges on one credit card. 5. Each credit card, however, were an easy way to go into debt.

Edited

B. Identify the subject and verb in each sentence. Edit each paragraph so that the errors in subject–verb agreement are corrected. The first sentence has been done for you. Then reread the edited paragraph to make sure that the changes make sense.

> 1. Once a week, Amelia and Daniel shops for groceries. 2. Each of them make a list of foods to get at the store. 3. They also watches for sales in the newspaper. 4. Amelia, along with Daniel, plan the food budget and the menu for the week. 5. Then, either Daniel or Amelia go to the store to buy the food. 6. Everything on their list, however, are not always in the store.

Edited

Once a week, Amelia and Daniel shop for groceries.

Student Assignment

If you have a rough draft of your own that is ready for editing, look at it now to see if the verb tenses are consistent and the subject and verbs agree. If you don't have a rough draft, try writing one. Use the prewriting and drafting instructions in Chapters 1–6. Revise for organization (see Chapters 7–12) and style (Chapters 13–18). Edit for fragments and run-on sentences (Chapter 19). Finally, check for consistency of verb tenses and subject–verb agreement.

Editing Checklist

After you have edited your rough draft, discuss your writing with your teacher or another person. Use the checklist as a guide.

1. Did I use verb tenses correctly to show when the action happened?

2. Did I avoid shifting back and forth between the present tense and the past tense?

3. Did I use singular verbs with singular subjects and plural verbs with plural subjects?

4. In sentences with two subjects joined by *or, nor,* or *but also,* did the verb agree with the nearer subject?

5. Did I use the singular form of the verb with words such as *everybody* and *everything?*

Video Replay

In the video, Sharon writes for voter registration forms so that she can vote in the next local election. Why is it important to vote in local elections? Write your thoughts and share your writing with another person.

ON YOUR OWN

Checking for Problems with Pronouns

VIDEO FOCUS

In the video, Jerry helps his wife Connie edit a rough draft of her letter to the electric company. She has used a **pronoun** incorrectly.

Pronouns are short words that help a writer avoid repeating other words, and make writing flow more smoothly. For a piece of writing to make a good impression, however, the pronouns must be used correctly.

Chapter Objectives

After seeing the video and completing this chapter, you will understand how to

- use the correct forms of subject pronouns, object pronouns, and possessive pronouns
- use singular pronouns with singular nouns or pronouns
- use plural pronouns with plural nouns or pronouns
- make pronouns agree in sex with nouns and pronouns they refer to
- avoid incorrect changes of pronouns (switching pronouns).

Key Words

Here are some important words that appear in this chapter and on the video. If you come across a word that does not occur in this list, write it down and ask your teacher to explain it to you.

pronoun	possessive pronoun
subject pronoun	singular
object pronoun	plural

Lesson 1 USING THE SUBJECT PRONOUNS CORRECTLY

Read the following paragraph aloud.

> Roberto is the salesman that you met at the block party. Roberto drives many miles every week. Tina, his wife, helps keep the car clean. Every week, Tina vacuums the floors, while Delia and I wash the outside. Delia and I do a good job, so Roberto and Tina are pleased. Roberto and Tina pay us well for our work.

This paragraph sounds boring because several words are repeated: *Roberto, Tina, Delia, I,* and *Tina.* These words are subjects for verbs in the sentences in which they appear.

Replacing some of these subject nouns with pronouns will improve the paragraph. In the edited version that follows, the **subject pronouns** are in boldface. Read the paragraph aloud. Notice that the sentences flow more smoothly.

> Roberto is the salesman that you met at the block party. **He** drives many miles every week. Tina, his wife, helps keep the car clean. Every week, **she** vacuums the floors, while Delia and I wash the outside. **We** do a good job, so Roberto and Tina are pleased. **They** pay us well for our work.

In the edited paragraph, you see the subject pronouns **he, she, we,** and **they**. Other subject pronouns are **it, you,** and **who**. Like subject nouns, subject pronouns usually come before the verbs in sentences.

All the subject pronouns in the edited paragraph about Roberto replace or refer to nouns that are subjects. For instance, *he* in the second sentence refers to Roberto, the subject of the first sentence. *She* in the fourth sentence refers to Tina, the subject of the third sentence. However, *you use a subject pronoun when the pronoun is the subject of a verb in a sentence, whether the word it refers to is a subject or not.*

In the following paragraph, all the subject pronouns refer to nouns in earlier sentences which are not subjects. (The subject pronouns are in boldface, and the nouns they refer to and replace are in parentheses right after them.)

> Training was provided for the new bus drivers. **They** (bus drivers) were taught many skills, including how to turn a corner. Learning was easy for one trainee. **He** (one trainee) was used to driving a large truck. I hope that the bus company will hire my friend and me, who both were trainees. **We** (my friend and me) both like driving and would like to get paid for it.

Lesson 2   USING OBJECT PRONOUNS CORRECTLY

The **object pronouns** are **me, you, him, her, it, us, them**. (Notice that *you* and *it* are both object pronouns and subject pronouns.) Object pronouns refer to nouns which are objects. There are two kinds of objects. One kind of object is a word that receives the action of a verb, as in "she told *us*." The other kind of object is a noun that is connected to *a preposition*, a word such as **before, after, with, on, about, by,** or **at.** In the following paragraph, the pronouns in the groups of words, "with *it*" and "with *him*," are object prounouns. Read the paragraph, and notice the object pronouns (in boldface), and the words they refer to and replace (which are in parentheses right after each pronoun).

> Dina's small engagement party made **her** (Dina) very happy. Her sister, Celia, surprised **her** (Dina) with **it** (the party). All six guests helped to make a cake. **We** (the six guests) put fifteen candles on **it** (the cake), one for each month Dina had been engaged. At the party, Dina blew **them** (the candles) out. Later, she told **us** (the six guests) about how she met Joe. We could tell she was in love with **him** (Joe) from the way she talked about **him** (Joe).

Notice that the object pronouns all come either right after verbs, or right after the prepositions, *with, on,* or *about.*

If you always use a subject pronoun when the pronoun is the subject of its sentence or clause, you will avoid one common mistake. That mistake is to use an object pronoun as the subject of a sentence or clause. There is an object pronoun to match every subject pronoun. Look at these two lists for a quick review.

subject pronoun	*object pronoun*
I	me
you	you
he	him
she	her
it	it
we	us
they	them

To use pronouns correctly, you must not mix up these two kinds of pronouns. For example, sometimes people use *me* when they should use *I*. *I*, not *me*, is always used as the subject. "*Delia and me* wash the car every week" is incorrect, because you would not say or write, "*Me* wash the car every week." Instead, you would say, "*I* wash the car every week." So you would say, "Delia and *I* wash the car every week." If one of the words in your subject is a pronoun, you can find out if it is correct by reading your sentence with the pronoun alone.

However, when you refer to yourself as the object, use *me*. It is incorrect to write "The bus company will hire *my friend and I*," because *I* is a subject pronoun. The *bus company* is the subject of the verb *hire*. The pronoun comes *after* the verb in the sentence, so you should use the object pronoun, *me*.

PRACTICE

Each sentence in the following paragraph offers you a choice (in boldface) between correct and incorrect subject pronouns. Rewrite the paragraph with the correct pronoun form. Then reread aloud the edited paragraph to make sure the changes make sense. The first sentence has been done for you.

Skip Sullivan, Joe Wysocki, and **I/me** got the flu. **We/Us** went to the company physician, Dr. Alberta Santos. **She/Her** prescribed some medicine. It gave Joe a headache. **He/Him** told Dr. Santos about it. **She/Her** changed the medicine. Skip and **I/Me** did not have any side effects from the medicine. **We/Us** were told to continue to take it.

Edited

Skip Sullivan, Joe Wysocki, and I got the flu.

Unit 4 Editing and Sharing

Lesson 3   USING POSSESSIVE PRONOUNS CORRECTLY

My, her, his, its, our, their, and **your** are called **possessive pronouns**. Possessive pronouns show belonging or ownership. A possessive pronoun describes what belongs to someone and who owns it. Look at these examples.

I like **Susan's** coat.
I like **her**   coat.

The possessive pronoun, *her*, placed before *coat*, tells you what belongs to Susan and that Susan owns the coat. *Her* replaces, or is used instead of, the possessive noun, *Susan's*. Look at these other examples of possessive pronouns used in place of possessive nouns.

He is **Carl's and my** doctor. I stepped on   **the dog's**   tail.
He is **our**   doctor. I stepped on   **its**   tail.

Carl is **George's**   father. That street is the **Thompson's** street.
Carl is **his**   father. That street is   **their**   street.

Possessive pronouns are also used to show possession by referring to other pronouns. The other pronouns always come before them in the sentence. The possessive pronouns always must agree with these other pronouns in number and sex.

I earn **my** pay.   **He** likes **his** dog.
You pay **your** taxes each year.   **She** combs **her** hair.
We bought **our** house last
year.   **It** (the car) lost **its** right rear wheel.
They sell **their** products.

In the following paragraph, the possessive pronouns (in boldface) replace the possessive nouns (in parentheses). You can see how many of the same words the writer would have had to use if the possessive pronouns had not been used instead. Knowing how to use possessive pronouns correctly and clearly will help to make your writing flow more smoothly.

Lisa and Carl celebrated **their** (Lisa's and Carl's) first wedding anniversary last week. Carl bought her a new dog as a present. **Its** (the dog's) tail and feet were white and **its** (the dog's) body was brown. Lisa told Carl that **her** (Lisa's) mother wanted to see **their** (Lisa's and Carl's) new pet. **Her** (Lisa's) mother had lost **her** (Lisa's mother's) pet dog recently. **Her** (Lisa's mother's) pet had been very old, and **its** (Lisa's mother's dog's) heart had failed. Carl liked **his** (Carl's) mother-in-law, and was glad to help her. He said they should ask **their** (his and Lisa's) friends where to find a puppy.

When you write, make sure you use pronouns carefully and clearly. In the following sentence, for example, who is buying the sewing machine?

Amelia went with Anna to buy **her** sewing machine.

Her could refer to either Amelia or Anna. Sometimes moving a pronoun closer to the word it refers to will make the meaning clearer. If Amelia is buying the sewing machine, here is a clearer way to write the sentence.

Amelia went to buy **her** sewing machine with Anna.

If Anna is buying the sewing machine, the sentence should be written like this:

Anna went to buy **her** sewing machine with Amelia.

Possessive pronouns often refer to nouns and pronouns that come before them in a sentence. When *Amelia* is placed before *her* in a the sentence, *her* refers to *Amelia*. When *Anna* is placed before *her* in the sentence, *her* refers to *Amelia*.

PRACTICE

Each sentence in the following paragraph offers you a choice (in boldface) between correct and incorrect possessive pronouns. Edit the paragraph for correct pronouns. Then reread the edited paragraph to make sure your choices make sense. The first sentence has been done for you.

Women who use birth-control pills should know about the added risks to **her/their** health. A 35-year-old women friend of mine smokes and has high blood pressure. She definitely should talk to **her/their** doctor before taking the pill. Another friend, James, knows that **her/his** wife, a heavy smoker, wants to use the pill. He is aware of **her/its/their** side effects on smokers. **His/her/their** doctor recommended another kind of birth control. If a woman wants to use the pill, she should learn about **her/their/its** possible harmful effects.

Edited

Women who use birth-control pills should know about the added risk to their health.

Lesson 4 MAKING PRONOUNS AGREE

Read the following pair of sentences.

> The woman opened **its** lunch box. **He** unwrapped a sandwich and ate **them**.

These sentences are confusing. The reader can't tell who owns the lunch box, why it was a man who unwrapped the sandwich, or how many sandwiches were eaten. The sentences should be corrected to read:

> The woman opened **her** lunch box. **She** unwrapped a sandwich and ate **it**.

To make the corrections, the writer asked the following questions about the noun each pronoun refers to.

- Is it male, female, or something that is neither male nor female (neuter)?
  This gives information about sex—male, female, or neuter. In the preceding example, the lunch box belonged to the woman, so the sentence should have read "The woman opened *her* lunch box." The woman unwrapped and ate the sandwich, so the second sentence needs to begin with *she*.
- Is it one person (or thing) or more than one?
  This gives information about number—singular or plural. In the preceding example, there is only one sandwich, so the pronoun referring to it should be singular and neuter: *it*.

When a pronoun replaces or refers to a noun or another person, the words should agree in sex and number. A singular pronoun is used with a singular noun, and a plural pronoun is used with a plural noun. **He, his**, or **him** is used when referring to one male. **She** or **her** is used when referring to one female. **It** or **its** is singular and does not refer to people, but only to things and places. **We, they, us, them, our**, and **their** are plural, and can be either male or female. **They, them**, and **their** are also used to refer to things which are neither male or female (neuter), such as cities, books, and plants.

In the following sentences, pronouns are boldface italics and underlined, and the nouns are in boldface.

Joan said, "I am taking **_my_** car."
Carl said, "I am taking **_my_** car."

(*My* is female or male, depending on who is speaking or who the *I* in the sentence is.)

You need **_your_** friends, he told me/him/her.
You need **_your_** friends, he told the group.

(*You* and *your* are the same for singular and plural, male and female.)

Barney hurried into the cafeteria, where **_he_** ate **_his_** lunch.

(*He* and *his* are singular pronouns that refer to **Barney**.)

George is my friend, so I loaned **_him_** my bicycle.

(*Him* is a singular pronoun referring to *George*.)

Lurleen went to the cafeteria, where **_she_** ate **_her_** lunch.

(*She* and *her* are singular pronouns that refer to *Lurleen*.)

George met his **mother** and gave **_her_** some money.

(*Her* is a singular pronoun referring to *mother*.)

Carlos and I strolled into the cafeteria, where **_we_** ate **_our_** lunches.
Georgia, Paul, and **I** went to the cafeteria, where **_we_** ate **_our_** lunch.

(*We* and *our* are plural pronouns that refer to two people, Carlos and I, and to three people, *Georgia, Paul*, and *I*. We and *our* are used for plurals which are male or female, or both.)

When **Carl** and **I** ate our lunch, they served ***us*** meatloaf.
When **Sue** and **I** ate lunch, they served ***us*** spaghetti.

(*Us* refers to two pairs of people, *Carl and I*, and *Sue and I*, which includes a male, *Carl*, and a female, *Sue*, and *I*, which may be either male or female. *Us* can be male or female, or both.)

The **workers** rushed into the cafeteria where ***they*** ate ***their*** lunches.

(*They* and *their* are plural pronouns that refer to **workers**. *They* and *their* can be male or female, or both.)

Carla asked **Mr. Sanchez** for **some napkins**. ***He*** gave ***them*** to ***her***.

(*He* is a singular pronoun that refers to *Mr. Sanchez. Them* is a plural pronoun that refers to *some napkins. Her* is a singular pronoun that refers to one female, *Carla*.)

Certain pronouns, such as **everyone, everybody, someone, somebody, no one, nobody, anyone, anybody, each, either**, and **neither** are *always singular*, and any pronouns referring to them must also be singular and must agree with them in sex.

Everyone in the group of waiters buys ***his*** own uniform.
Everyone in the group of waitresses buys ***her*** own uniform.
Everyone in the school band buys ***his or her*** own uniform.

(We use *his or her* because we don't know the sex of the band members.)

Each of the women cares for ***her*** own children.
Each of the men took ***his*** children to the game.
Neither of the new workers has ***his or her*** time card.

(We use *his or her* if we don't know the sex of the new workers, or if one of them is male and one of them is female.)

Everything in the workshop is in ***its*** place.

(We use *its* because *everything* is neuter—neither male nor female.)

Also, when **or** or **nor** joins two subjects, the pronoun following the subjects agrees in number and sex with the subject closer to it.

Neither the plumbers nor the **painter** took ***his or her*** break.

(We use *his or her* because we don't know the sex of the painter, and the pronoun must agree with the closer subject: *Painter* is singular.)

Neither the plumbers nor the **painters** took ***their*** break.

(*Their* refers to *painters*, which is plural.)

Either Jack or **Jane** drove ***her*** car.

(*Her* agrees with *Jane*, the subject closer to the pronoun.)

Either Jane or **Jack** drove ***his*** car.

(*His* agrees with Jack, the subject closer to the pronoun.)

PRACTICE

In each sentence in the following paragraph, choose the correct pronoun. Then reread the edited paragraph to make sure the changes make sense. The first sentence has been done for you.

Charlene was bored with _____ job as a cook in the Quick Stop Cafe. Linda, a waitress, was unhappy where _____ worked. Charlene read that Mr. Cole, the owner of a new restaurant, was hiring employees. _____ needed a cook and some waitresses. Each of the women wanted to leave _____ job. However, neither of them wanted to quit until _____ had a job at the new restaurant. Charlene and Linda decided to continue where they were until the new restaurant offered _____ work.

Edited

Charlene was bored with her job as a cook in the Quick Shop Cafe.

Lesson 5 · AVOIDING INCORRECT CHANGES OF PRONOUNS (SWITCHING PRONOUNS)

Read the following sentences.

> ***Somebody*** may work hard to save ***his or her*** money.
> Then ***they*** find out prices have gone up and things cost more.

The passage begins by using the pronouns *he or she* to refer to *somebody*, but then the second sentence switches to the pronoun *they*. In general, you should continue to use the same pronoun when you are referring to the same noun or pronoun that comes before it. Switching pronouns is incorrect and sometimes confusing. Switching pronouns is often a problem when writing more than one sentence. The correct form of the sentences is:

> ***Somebody*** may work hard to save ***his or her*** money.
> Then ***he or she*** finds out prices have gone up and things cost more.

Note: You can avoid using *he or she* by changing the noun or pronoun referred to from singular to plural. Often, people use the plural in speaking and writing to avoid using *he or she*.

> ***Some people*** may work hard to save ***their*** money.
> Then ***they*** find out prices have gone up and things cost more.

Switching pronouns is most likely to happen when you are writing several sentences on the same topic. Look at these sentences.

> **Most people** enjoy Thanksgiving. ***They*** get together with friends and family and celebrate. ***We*** all eat a big, delicious turkey.

The corrected form of the sentences would be:

> **Most people** enjoy Thanksgiving. **_They_** get together with friends and family and celebrate. **_They_** all eat a big, delicious turkey.

Switching from another pronoun to *you* is common both in single sentences and with several sentences. Look at these examples.

Incorrect: As *we* started the car, *you* could hear a loud grinding.
Correct: As *we* started the car, *we* could hear a loud grinding.

Incorrect: If *someone* wants to run for a union office, *he or she* must be nominated. To get nominated, *you* must be popular.
Correct: If someone wants to run for a union office, *he or she* must be nominated. To get nominated, *he or she* must be popular.

Switching pronouns is a common mistake in writing. You should check everything you write to make sure you have not made this error. Changing pronouns in this way is sometimes confusing, and even when your meaning is clear, your writing will be incorrect and make a poor impression if it contains this mistake.

PRACTICE

There are incorrect changes of pronoun in the following paragraph. Edit the paragraph to correct the switching of pronouns. Then reread the edited paragraph to see if the pronouns you have used make sense throughout and are the best choices you could make.

Many people use the Yellow Pages in the telephone book to find a job. If people want to sell women's clothes in a store, you can look up the subject *Clothing* in the Yellow Pages. They also can find references to related subjects you are interested in, including *Sportswear—Retail* and *Women's Apparel—Retail*. You may call the store managers and ask if you need a salesclerk. Some of the managers will say that we want to arrange an interview. If they use the Yellow Pages, a person may find a number of leads for a job.

Edited

_____

_____

_____

_____

REVIEW EXERCISE

Edit the following paragraph for pronoun use. As you read each sentence, identify the pronouns. Then decide whether the pronoun is used correctly or incorrectly. Replace incorrect pronouns with correct ones. There are five errors in all. You may need to change some words to make the meaning clear. Reread the edited paragraph to be sure that all the corrections make sense.

The apartment building is losing many of their tenants because of several problems. Neither the tenants nor the landlord are able to stop drug-selling in the hallways. When loose plaster falls on tenants, you can be hurt. A tenant named Edward Robinson and his wife, Marlene, are running for positions in the Tenants' Association. Him and Marlene will present some solutions to the problems at the Association meeting. Some other tenants are also running for office. After everyone casts their vote, the votes will be counted. The winner will be the President of the Association.

Edited

_____

_____

_____

_____

_____

Student Assignment

If you have a rough draft of your own that is ready for editing, look at it now to see if you have used pronouns correctly. If you don't have a rough draft, try writing one. Use the prewriting and drafting instructions in Chapter 1–6. Revise for organization (see Chapters 7–12) and style (Chapters 13–18). Edit for fragments and run-on sentences (Chapter 19). Check for consistency of verb tenses and subject–verb agreement (Chapter 20). Finally, make sure you have used pronouns correctly.

Edited Checklist

After you have edited your rough draft, discuss your writing with your teacher or another person. Use the checklist as a guide.

1. Did I use the correct forms of pronouns?
2. Do the pronouns refer clearly to nouns or other pronouns?
3. Does each pronoun agree in number and sex with the word it refers to?
4. Have I avoided making incorrect changes of pronoun (switching pronouns)?

Video Replay

In the video, Connie is editing a letter she has written to the electric company about an error on her bill. Have you ever found an error on a bill? Write about what you did and how you felt. Share your writing with another person.

ON YOUR OWN

CHAPTER 22 *EDITING*

Checking for Spelling Errors

VIDEO FOCUS

In the video, Tommy helps his son check his science report for spelling errors. By reading the report backwards, word for word, they catch a careless error. They also find an incorrectly spelled homonym. Although this word sounds right, it is spelled differently because it has a different meaning from the word his son intended to write.

Incorrect spelling may cause a reader to misunderstand the writer's message or have a negative reaction to the writing. Correct spelling shows the reader that the writer cares about his or her writing. In the editing stage of the writing process, professional writers use dictionaries or computerized spell-checks to make sure their words are spelled correctly.

Chapter Objectives

After seeing the video and completing this chapter, you will understand how

- to correct common errors made in the endings of words
- to choose the homonym with the meaning you want
- to find spelling errors by using a special method.

Key Words

Here are some important words that appear in this chapter or on the video. Read the definitions of them under the list below. If you need further explanation, ask your teacher.

consonant   vowel
syllable   homonym
accent

A **syllable** is a part of a word that makes a separate sound. The word *paper* has two syllables, *pa-* and *-per*. *Saturday* has three syllables: *Sat-ur-day*. When we speak a word, we emphasize one syllable more than any other, which is called the **accented** or **stressed syllable**. The emphasis or **accent** is shown by a slanted mark over the stressed syllable, as in *páper* or *Sáturday*. All the sounds in words are made up of letters of the alphabet which are either vowels or consonants. The **vowels** are: *a, e, i, o,* or *u.* All the other letters of the alphabet are **consonants**.

Homonyms are words that sound exactly alike but have different meanings and are spelled differently. You will study them in this chapter.

Lesson 1   SPOTTING COMMON SPELLING PROBLEMS

The following rules can help you locate and correct common spelling problems. The words are underlined. The part of the word you should pay special attention to is shown in boldface.

1. In a one-syllable verb which ends in a consonant, you double the final consonant.

    <u>Sto**p**</u> trouble before it starts.
    She <u>sto**pped**</u> smoking before she became pregnant.
    <u>Sto**pping**</u> a bad habit takes repeated effort.

    He wants to <u>**fit**</u> in with the new crowd.
    The man at the store <u>**fitted**</u> my new coat for me.
    My mother is <u>**fitting**</u> all my clothes for my younger brother.

    (In the video, Tommy's son found a spelling error of this kind in his paper. He had spelled the -ing form of *get* as *geting* instead of *getting*.)

2. In a verb of more than one syllable, if the last syllable is accented and the word has a final consonant, double the final consonant.

> Con-tról your child's behavior in public.
> The parents contrólled their children's table manners in the restaurant.
> They are contrólling the way the children act toward storekeepers.
>
> If you re-fér to page 12, you will see how to assemble this toy.
> By reférring to the manual, I was able to assemble the toy.
> I reférred to the manual, which gave clear directions.

3. When a verb ends in a silent **-e**, drop the **-e** before adding **-ing**. To form the past tense, add a **-d**.

> I rake leaves every fall.
> Raking leaves is good exercise.
> I raked leaves last fall.
>
> The Garcias invite you to the movies whenever they go.
> They are inviting all their neighbors tonight.
> Mr. Garcia also invited his coworkers.
>
> When I eat too fast, I choke.
> If I am choking on food, the Heimlich maneuver helps.
> I choked last night on a piece of meat.

4. When **-y** is the last letter in a word and the **-y** is preceded by a consonant, change the **-y** to **-i** before adding **-es** or **-ed**.

> Apply for a new job if you don't like the job you have.
> Anita applies for any job she is able to do.
> She applied for the job of bank teller last week.
>
> Here at Joe's Diner, we fry seafood.
> We serve french fries.
> If you like fried food, eat at Joe's Diner.
>
> My friend is going to have a baby.
> Yesterday, her doctor said she would have two babies—twins!
> At dinner, her husband babied her.
>
> The president of the company met with the employees.
> Two companies in town were considering new health plans.

The Legal Aid lawyers <u>accompany</u> clients to court.
Julio's lawyer <u>accompanies</u> him to all court appearances.
She <u>accompanied</u> him to the sentencing this morning.

5. When the noun ends in **-ch, -s, -ss, -sh,** or **-x,** add **-es** to make it plural. The **-es** ending is pronounced as an extra syllable.

I like to go to <u>the church</u> in my neighborhood.
My town has three <u>churches</u>.
I take <u>the bus</u> to work.
Two <u>buses</u> came to my stop.
Tawana decided to buy <u>the red dress</u>.
She had tried on several <u>dresses</u> first.

Make <u>a wish</u> before you blow out the candles on your birthday cake.
Kevin made <u>two wishes</u>, one for happiness and one for health.

The screws are in <u>the box</u>.
<u>Two boxes</u> of screws are on the shelf.

6. When **-i** and **-e** appear next to each other in a word, place the **-i** before **-e** except after **-c**.

A **piece** of bread is all I want.
The **thief** was caught.
The fire **chief** suspected that arson caused the fire.
They be<u>lie</u>ve their team will win.

I <u>receive</u> a call from my mother once a day.
I will not <u>deceive</u> my doctor about what I eat.

Memorize the *exceptions to the rule*, such as **neighbor, weigh, their, foreign, neither**, and **either**. One way to memorize a list of words is to make up a sentence with them. Here is a sentence for this list.

If for**ei**gn n**ei**ghbors w**ei**gh th**ei**r choices, they may like **ei**ther or n**ei**ther.

The following paragraphs contain underlined words. Some of these words are misspelled. In each paragraph, correct the errors as you rewrite the paragraph. The first error in each paragraph has been corrected for you.

1. **Hint:** In the following paragraph, verbs with an **-ed** or **-ing** ending need a double consonant.

   1. Luisa was upset with herself for **leting** her temper get out of hand. 2. **Droping** a plate and then **geting** angry **stired** up trouble with everyone. 3. Several customers had not **tiped** her as much as usual because of her behavior. 4. She **hoped** everyone was **forgeting** the whole thing. 5. **Admiting** her mistake, Luisa **beged** forgiveness from the steady customers she had insulted. 6. The customers never **refered** to the incident again, so she **stoped freting**.

2. **Hint:** In the following paragraph, make the necessary corrections in the underlined verbs. For the two verbs in parentheses, write the correct **-ing** form.

   1. There are three benefits of **exerciseing** strenuously at least three times weekly for half an hour each time. 2. (**Reduce**) the risk of a heart attack is a major result. 3. You will also find yourself **copeing** better with mental and physical stress. 4. In addition, (**like**) your body will give you a good feeling about yourself. 5. You may exercise by **skateing, hiking**, and folk **danceing** and have fun at the same time.

Edited

There are three benefits of exercising strenuously at least three times weekly for half an hour each time.

3. **Hint:** In the following paragraph, endings have been added to words that end in a **-y** preceded by a consonant. Sometimes the **-y** has not been changed before the ending when it should be. Sometimes the ending is correct.

1. My neighborhood has had several **tragedys** in recent months. 2. Robbers **pryed** open the doors of several houses and stole many TVs. 3. Two **secretarys** had a fire in their apartment. 4. Our block association **tried** to think of ways to prevent such problems. 5. The association also made a plan for dealing with **emergencys**. 6. In the practice fire drills, we **emptyed** our apartment building in ten minutes.

Edited

My neighborhood has had several tragedies in recent months.

4. **Hint:** The following paragraph contains nouns with incorrect plurals. Some nouns do not have **-es** endings when they should. Other nouns have **-es** endings when they should not.

1. The picnic **lunches** were served on checkered **tablecloths**. 2. Plastic **dishs** and **forkes** were provided. 3. The tables were decorated with **bunchs** of grapes. 4. Someone had made several **batchs** of tuna. 5. For dessert, there was cake made from **mixs**. 6. After the picnic, the **guestes** wrote their names and **address** on a list.

Edited

The picnic lunches were served on checkered tableclothes.

5. **Hint:** You can correct the misspelled words in the following paragraph if you remember that **-i** usually comes before **-e** except after **-c**. Check all words in a dictionary, as there may be exceptions.

1. **Greif** is a common reaction to the death of a loved one. 2. This feeling may be **breif** or last for years. 3. At the **height** of **thier** pain, people may feel **feirce** anger. 4. They may **percieve** life as cruel. 5. An understanding **freind** is a great comfort. 6. In time, most people **queitly** accept their loss.

Edited

Grief is a common reaction to the death of a loved one.

6. **Hint:** Several different kinds of spelling errors appear in the next paragraph.

> 1. One night, the **theif hurryed** into the department store. 2. First, she stole three **peices** of jewelry and four **boxs** of **watchs**. 3. Next, she took four **foriegn dresss**. 4. She **planed** on stealing more items, but the night watchman **stoped** her. 5. He **accompanyed** the **theif** to the police **cheif**, who booked her for petty larceny.

Edited

One night, the thief hurried into the department store.

Lesson 2   SPELLING HOMONYMS CORRECTLY

Homonyms are words that sound exactly alike but have different meanings and different spellings. Some word pairs are commonly confused. Be sure that you use the correct homonym so that you do not confuse your audience.

your–you're

The top portion of a bill is **your** receipt (the receipt that belongs to you).
We hope that **you're** (you are) going to feel better soon.

(On the video this homonym error is one of the spelling mistakes Tommy's son finds in his paper.)

their–there–they're

The waiters and waitresses washed **their** hands (the hands belonging to themselves) before they served the meals.
But the new shipment of stereos **there** (in that place) by the trucks.
Roberto and Heraldo told me that **they're** (they are) pleased with the new sick leave policy.

its–it's

The car was damaged in an accident. **Its** (the car's) bumper was badly smashed.
It's (it is) a good job if you like to work with heavy equipment.

to–too–two

Go **to** (toward) the personnel office.
Get a job application **to** fill out (verb form).
Carlos should go, **too** (also).
I ate the rice and beans first because the enchilada was still **too** (overly) hot.
Mr. Hernandez gave us **two** (2) tickets for the baseball game.

weather–whether

I don't know **whether** (if) he'll come.
We go swimming in the hot **weather** (conditions of temperature, wind, rain, sun, etc.)

whose–who's

I wonder **whose** (which person's) lunch was left on the table.
Who's (who is) bringing the salad to the picnic?

passed–past

I **passed** (did well enough) on the test.
I **passed** (went by) four stalled cars.
In the **past** (time before now), I made my own clothes.

peace–piece

Many people volunteer their time and donate money to organizations that promote **peace** (absence of war).
Would you like a **piece** (a part) of fruit for dessert?

right–write

Please show me the **right** (correct) way to iron these skirts.
In the drawer on the **right** (direction opposite to left) you will find stamps and envelopes.
I wish I could see you **right** now (at once).
If you do not support the increased taxes, **write** (send a letter) to your senators and express your opinion.

by–buy

Will you please wait for me **by** (near) the post office?
By (through the act of) checking the ads, you can find bargains.
Please be home **by** (not later than) 6 P.M.
Do you want to **buy** (purchase) frozen corn or canned peas?

hear–here

Please **hear** (listen to) our grievances.
Stand and speak loudly so that everyone can **hear** (know what words you are saying).
If you want to get a ride on the downtown bus, wait **here** (in this place) next to the bus sign.

hole–whole

The cigarette burned a **hole** (opening) in the chair.
The hungry guests ate a **whole** (entire) bowl of tortilla chips with salsa before dinner.

know–no

Do you **know** (understand) how to repair a sewing machine?
Do you **know** (recognize) this man?
With your bad cold, you are in **no** (not any) condition to go to work.
No (negative response), I do not want to take a taxi.

knew–new

Because he had previous work experience in doing inventories, he already **knew** (past tense of know) how to fill out the shipment forms.
Last month we bought **new** (unused) curtains for the apartment.

PRACTICE

In the following paragraph, choose the correct homonyms from the words in parentheses. Then rewrite the paragraph with the correct homonym. Check the meanings in this book or in a dictionary. The first sentence has been corrected for you.

1. The hostess offered me a (**peace/piece**) of strawberry pie for (**desert/dessert**). 2. Just (**buy/by**) looking at the whipped cream, I (**knew/new**) that the pie had (**to/too/two**) many calories for my diet. 3. (**Its/It's**) hard for me to stop at just one bite. 4. I would probably end up eating the (**hole/whole**) thing. 5. In the end, I saw that (**their/there/they're**) was only one (**right/write**) choice. 6. I refused the pie and all (**its/it's**) calories. 7. After all, (**whose/who's**) body will get fat if I eat the pie?

Edited

The hostess offered me a piece of strawberry pie for dessert.

Finding Spelling Errors

Spelling errors are often missed when you read from beginning to end because your mind supplies the missing letters or ignores the incorrect ones. You can find many misspelled words by reading an entire paragraph backwards, word by word. As you look at each word, check the spelling. After you have read the paragraph backwards slowly, word by word, check the corrections by reading the paragraph forward. Be sure that you have used the correct homonyms.

REVIEW EXERCISES

In the following two paragraphs, you will find many spelling errors. Read each paragraph backward, word by word, and correct the spelling errors. Remember to check for the right homonym. Be sure your corrections make sense when you read the edited paragraph backward.

1. Makeing a budget is easy if you no the basic procedure. 2. First, right down all of you're income for one month. 3. Income means all of the money you recieve, including your paycheck and any other checkes from Social Security and the government. 4. Next, figure out your regular monthly expenses. 5. Rent and utilitys are regular monthly expenses. 6. Food billes should be included to. 7. Third, list special expenses, such as doctors, gifts, repair costs, and clothing that change from month to month. 8. Buy prepareing a budget, you can tell how much money too put in your savings account. 9. You can tell which special expenses should not be incured until later.

1. Its important to find the write apartment for you and you're family. 2. Their are real estate agencys and newspaper ads that can help you to find one. 3. Before you look at apartments, decide what part of town you want to live in. 4. You may want to live near the bus lines, buy churchs, or close to work. 5. When you look at the apartment, right down the landlord's name and phone number, the address of the apartment, and the price of the rent. 6. Find out weather the utilitys are included and whether they're is a security deposit. 7. As you inspect the apartment, look for repaires that are needed, such as wholes in the walls or peaces of floor tiles. 8. Its also important to no about any restrictions such as ownning pets or haveing children in the apartment. 9. Before you sign the lease, be sure to read it carefully and understand it's conditions.

_____

_____

_____

_____

Student Assignment

If you are editing a rough draft, check it now for spelling errors by reading the draft backwards, word by word. Check for incorrect homonyms. If you don't have a rough draft, try writing one. Use the prewriting and drafting instructions in Chapters 1–6. Revise for organization (see Chapters 7–12) and style (Chapters 13–18). Edit for fragments and run-on sentences (Chapter 19), subject–verb agreement and consistency of tenses (Chapter 20), and pronoun agreement (Chapter 21). Finally, correct spelling errors. Make sure you check your corrections by reading the paragraph forward.

Revising Checklist

After you have edited your rough draft, discuss your writing with your teacher or another person. Use the checklist as a guide.

1. Did I find spelling errors by reading my paragraph backwards, word by word?
2. Did I check my writing for the common spelling errors listed in this chapter?
3. Did I use the correct homonym for the meaning I wanted?

Video Replay

In the video, Tommy's son is checking his report for science class. Newspapers and magazines often have articles with science. What scientific topics interest you? Medicine, space exploration, ocean life, diet research, nuclear energy, or computer technology? Write about some topic in science that interests you. Share your writing with another person.

ON YOUR OWN

CHAPTER 23 *EDITING*

Checking for Punctuation and Capitalization

VIDEO FOCUS

In the video, Tony helps his son Luis correct a letter Luis has written about why he wants to go to college. Luis's errors in punctuation and capitalization make his writing confusing and give a poor impression of him.

When you speak, you communicate part of your meaning by pausing, by raising or lowering your voice, and by emphasizing certain words. This helps listeners tell when a thought begins or ends and what information is important. In writing, you need to use punctuation and capitalization to help readers understand your meaning.

Chapter Objectives

After seeing the video and completing this chapter, you will understand how to

- punctuate the ends of five kinds of sentences
- use commas to make thoughts clear within a sentence
- use apostrophes to show possession and to form contractions
- capitalize words in a sentence.

Key Words

Here are some important words that appear in this chapter or on the video. If you come across a new word that is not on this list, write it down and ask your teacher to explain it to you.

period   comma
question mark   contraction
exclamation point   apostrophe

Lesson 1   PUNCTUATING THE END OF A SENTENCE

1. Use a **period** at the end of **statement of fact**.

   The supervisor showed us how to check the inventory.
   At the library, many books on home repair are available.
   If I get my work done, we can go to the movies.

2. Use a **period** at the end of a **command**. The subject of every command is an understood *you*.

   Buy a gallon of milk, please.
   Please stack the dishes next to the dishwasher.
   Come visit if you're in the neighborhood.

3. Use a **question mark** at the end of a **question**.

   Can Luis swim?
   Do you have experience driving a delivery truck?
   What time does the movie begin?

   When a question is asked in the form of a statement, as in the following example, it ends in a period.

   I want to know what time the movie begins.

4. Use an **exclamation point** at the end of a **strong command**. These are short, urgent sentences.

   Do it!
   Run for your life!
   Duck!

5. Use an **exclamation point** when you want to state a very strong feeling.

>They won the lottery!
>I'm not a liar!
>Your speech was terrific!

PRACTICE

Edit the following paragraph by inserting or correcting the punctuation at the end of each sentence. The first error has been corrected for you. Then read the edited paragraph to make sure the punctuation makes sense.

>Do you know how to carry out a job search! There are many actions you can take you should think big. Are you willing to retrain in a new industry. If you are a steelworker. Learn construction skills. Second, move to where the jobs are if you are a computer worker, move to California. Third, accept more responsibility. If you are an assembly worker. Study to be a supervisor! A job search can be an eye-opening experience there are a lot of choices you can consider! If you make the effort?

Editing

Do you know how to carry out a job search?

Lesson 2   PUNCTUATING A COMBINED SENTENCE

1. Use a **comma** when you join two independent clauses with *and, but, yet, so*, or *or*. The comma is placed at the end of the first sentence.

Sentence 1+Comma	Connector	Sentence 2
Thomas fixes dinner,	and	Theresa does the dishes.
Theresa dislikes cooking,	but	Thomas enjoys it.
Thomas tries a new recipe,	or	Theresa makes stew.
Thomas can't make desserts,	so	Theresa makes them.
Theresa knows that recipe,	yet	she never makes a meal from it.

2. Use a **comma** after a phrase with three or more words in it, or after a dependent clause if it appears at the beginning of a sentence.

With a carefully written resume, you can show the interviewer your qualifications.

During the interview, you can give more details of your experience.

Because many workplaces are now smoke-free, you may be asked about your smoking habits.

If you learn about the company, you will be able to decide whether to accept or refuse a job offer.

PRACTICE

A. Edit the following paragraph. Join the sentences on either side of each blank space by inserting a comma and **and, but, yet, so**, or **or**.

Rena decided to have a party on Saturday night _____ Nancy helped her plan it. At first, everybody said he or she would come _____ then one guest learned he had to work the night shift. Finding the perfect time was hard _____ Rena and Nancy did not know whether to have it or not. They could have the party without everybody _____ they could postpone the party until everyone could attend. Rena and Nancy stopped trying to find the perfect date _____ they went on with their plans for the party.

Edited

Rena decided to have a party on Saturday night, and Nancy helped her plan it.

B. Edit the following paragraph by inserting a comma after a phrase of three words or more, or after a dependent clause if it begins a sentence. The first sentence has been done for you.

When people work hard they get tired and need relaxation. If they don't find a way to relax they may resent going back to work. For suggestions on how different kinds of workers relax read the rest of this paragraph. Between days on an assembly line a worker might enjoy playing handball or reading a book. If you do physical labor for eight hours you might like to watch television. For a person who sits at a desk all day dancing is a good change of pace.

Edited

When people work hard, they get tired.

Lesson 3 PUNCTUATING A SERIES OF ITEMS

Use **commas** to separate three or more items in a series. The items in the series can be nouns, verbs, phrases, or dependent clauses. Look at the following sentences. Notice that if the word before the first item in the series applies to all the items, it does not have to be repeated in front of each item. For example, in the first sentence, it is clear that the chairs and windows the school bought are new, too, so the word *new* does not need to be repeated.

The school bought **new tables, chairs**, and **windows** for our room.

They invited **Carl, Luisa**, and **Martin** to the party.

His brother **hits, steals bases**, and **fields** better than anybody else on the team.

Cindy can **dance, sing**, and **play** the saxophone.

Magazines are sold **at newstands, in bookstores**, and **at supermarkets**.
The firemen fought the blaze **with water, foam spray**, and **axes**.

(*With* clearly applies to all the items, and need not be repeated.)

Kara is changing jobs **because her present position is boring, her salary is low**, and **her skills are in demand**.

(*Because* clearly applies to all the items, and need not be repeated.)

They will get married **if he finishes high school, gets a job**, and **saves some money**.

(**If** clearly applies to all the items, and need not be repeated.)

Nouns in a series which are the subject of a sentence *never* have a comma after the last item because you never put a comma between the subject and the verb of a sentence if the verb comes right after the subject.

Incorrect: The men, women, and children, came early.
Correct:

The men, women, and children came early.

PRACTICE

Edit the following paragraph by inserting commas in each sentence where they are needed. Eliminate any unnecessary words that are repeated in a series. The first sentence has been done for you.

Some advertisements make people want things that they don't need can't afford or don't have space for. Maybe your car is four years old runs well and looks okay. In an ad you see a sexy man or woman driving a Honda a Mercedes or a

Cadillac. The advertisers want you to believe that if you buy a new car you will be sexier you will be more popular and you will be happier. They want you to think you need a new car with a brand-new engine brand-new tires and brand-new seat covers. Sometimes the new car you buy makes you worry about the monthly payments on the job at home and at parties.

Edited

Some advertisements make people want things that they don't need, can't afford, or don't have space for.

REVIEW EXERCISE

Edit the following paragraph by inserting the nine commas that have been omitted and adding **and, but, or, yet**, or **so** in the blank spaces. The first sentence has been done for you.

I wrote to my landlord three times last year about the bad condition of my apartment _____ he has not answered once. The walls need scraping plastering and painting. After a heavy rainstorm the ceiling leaks. The wall stays damp a long time _____ the paint peels. When I take a shower plaster chips fall all over me. Because my letters have been ignored I plan to complain to the Housing Bureau the Health Department and the City Council. The landlord must repair my apartment soon _____ I will have to take stronger action.

Edited

I wrote to my landlord three times last year about the bad condition of my apartment, but he has not answered once.

Lesson 4   USING AN APOSTROPHE TO SHOW POSSESSION

Possessive forms of words show possession or ownership. With nouns, to show possession you use an **apostrophe**/s or an /s/**apostrophe**, as in these examples:

> The tall boy**'s** bicycle is green. *(apostrophe/s)*
>
> (The bicycle that belongs to the tall boy, or the bicycle that the tall boy owns, is green.)
>
> The two boy**s'** bicycles are new. *(s/apostrophepe)*
>
> (The bicycles that belong to the two boys, or the bicycles that the two boys own, are new.)

The main rule for showing possession with nouns is:

- If the noun does not end in an -**s** (as in **boy**), add an *apostrophe and an -s* to show possession, as in **boys.'**
- If the noun already ends in an -**s** (as in **boys**), add *only an apostrophe* after the final -**s** to show possession, as in **boys'**.

If you always remember this rule, you will punctuate possessive nouns correctly. The following rules may help you to follow this main rule.

1. Add -**'s** after singular nouns and after all the singular pronouns such as *everybody, anybody, someone, nobody* (for a full treatment of these pronouns, see Chapter 21, pages 223–24.)

> The driver**'s** jacket was covered with dust.
> Mrs. Smith**'s** mother is sick.
> Everyone**'s** overtime pay will be increased.

2. Add only an apostrophe with most plural nouns. Most plural nouns end in -**s**.

> The drivers**'** jackets were covered with dust.
> The Smiths**'** house is for sale.
> The cars**'** engines were dead.

3. If a plural noun does not end in -**s** you add **'s**.

> The children**'s** clothes fit them very well.
> The women**'s** group petitioned the government.

4. With plural nouns, you -'s or -s' only to show possessive. If you are only making a noun plural, you add only an -s.

> Maria ironed the skirt's. (incorrect)
> Maria ironed the skirts. (correct)

5. If two or more people possess a thing together, add an -'s only after the last person named.

> Vera and Pedro's house was burglarized. (They both own the same house.)
>
> BUT
>
> Vera's and Pedro's houses were burglarized. (Each person owns his or her own house. There are two houses owned by two people, and each of their names must show possession.)

PRACTICE

Edit the following paragraph by inserting an apostrophe in the underlined words to show possession. The first sentence has been edited for you. Then reread the edited paragraph to see if all your punctuation gives the meaning that you want.

Jack and **Mikes** Sporting Goods Store is having a sale. **Mens, womens,** and **childrens** jackets are a good buy. Because sale days are busy, the **stores** closing time has been extended to 9 P.M. For the **customers** convenience, **Jacks** and **Mikes** children are helping out. The **sales** have been greater than anyone expected.

Edited

Jack and Mike's Sporting Good Store is having a Sale.

Lesson 5 USING AN APOSTROPHE TO MAKE A CONTRACTION

A **contraction** is a shorter way of writing a group of words by combining two words into one word. For example, instead of writing *I am tired* you write *I'm tired*. You combine *I* and *am* and leave out the *a*. You put an apostrophe (') in place of the *a*. All contractions are formed by (a) combining two words, (b) leaving out one or more letters, and (c) replacing the letter(s) left out with an apostrophe ('). Almost all contractions combine a subject and a verb. Contractions are formed the same way with noun-subjects and pronoun-subjects. Look at the following examples. The letters left out of the contraction are underlined.

Completely Spelled-out Form	*Contraction Form*
I **am** worried about her.	I'm worried about her.
You **are** worried also.	You're worried also.
Their wages **are** higher.	Their wages're higher.
Who **is** going to do it?	Who's going to do it?
It **is** nice of you to help.	It's nice of you to help.
We **are** members of the team.	We're members of the team.
She **will** give us the key.	She'll give us the key.
The landlady can**not** fix it.	The landlady can't fix it.
They **have** been here since June.	They've been here since June.
The landlady should **have** come.	The landlady should've come.
The foreman could **have** seen it.	The foreman could've seen it.
Carl does **not** like his car.	Carl doesn't like his car.
We **would** like more security.	We'd like more security.

Notice that *could've* and *should've* are contractions of *could have* and *should have*, not *could of* and *should of*.

PRACTICE

A. Edit the following paragraph by changing all the boldface words into contractions. Because it is a letter written in everyday language to a friend, not in businesslike language, it is proper to use contractions in it. Use an apostrophe in place of the dropped letters. Then read aloud the edited paragraph to make sure the contractions make sense. The first sentence has been done for you.

> **I am** happy that **you are** enjoying your vacation. **It is** great that your friend is sharing it with you. Unfortunately, I **cannot** join you at the lake until next week because my car is in the shop. It **should not** need fixing so soon, but the

ignition **does not** work right. As soon as the car is fixed, **I will** come to see you.

Edited

I'm happy that you're enjoying your vacation.

B. Edit the following paragraph by spelling out the boldface contractions. The first sentence has been done for you.

Mr. and Mrs. Wilson **should've** registered their children at our school. They **couldn't** come at the regular time because Mrs. Wilson was in the hospital. **She'll** be home in a week. **We'd** like the Wilsons to complete the registration forms soon, but **we're** happy to accept the children now. The school closes at 3 P.M. Mr. Wilson **doesn't** get home from work until 6 P.M. The principal would like to know **who's** going to care for the children between 3 P.M. and 6 P.M.

Edited

Mr. and Mrs. Wilson should have registered their children at school.

Lesson 6   CAPITALIZING WORDS IN A SENTENCE

1. Capitalize the first word in a sentence.

   Beans are a good source of protein.

2. Capitalize the first and last names of a person and the name of a city, state, country, or geographical spot.

   Carmen Diaz (first and last name of a person) was born in **Mexico** (country). Now she lives in **St. Louis** (city), **Missouri** (state), near the **Mississippi River** (geographical spot).

3. Capitalize the name of a language, a nationality, and a religion.

Lise is Haitian and has been in the United States four years, so she speaks **French** and **English**. She and her friends Jean and Marie are **Catholic**, but her **American** husband is a **Baptist**.

4. Capitalize a person's official title when the name follows the title. Do not capitalize a general mention of that title.

Doctor Evans, **Representative** Donaldson, and **Judge** Mendoza called on **President** Smith and **Councilwoman** Saunders.

BUT

A group of **doctors, representatives**, and **judges** called on the **president** and a **councilwoman**.

5. Capitalize the names of businesses, newspapers, movies, and books.

At **Wardman's Drugstore**, you can buy **USA Today, People** and **Time** magazines, and paperback books like **The Catcher in the Rye**. Next door at the **Loew's Theater**, you can see Eddie Murphy in **Beverly Hills Cop V**.

PRACTICE

Edit the following paragraph by correcting all eight errors in capitalization. The first error has been corrected for you.

Some Doctors in albany, new York, including doctor Bruce johnson, tested a new cancer drug made by simmons drug company on their patients. The mayor of the city along the Hudson river thanked everyone for their participation. this drug was to be tested next in Rome, italy, where the participants will be french, american, and italian.

Edited

Some doctors

_____

_____

_____

_____

REVIEW EXERCISE

Edit the following paragraph by correcting all thirteen errors in punctuation and capitalization. When you have finished, reread the edited paragraph to make sure your corrections make sense.

The union leader, president Harris, should tell his members about a companys responsibility for it's workers? Its important for employees to know their rights. Companies like miller tool company must warn employees about anything on the job that might be dangerous, such as machines explosives and poisons! If workers are to do their jobs safely employers must give them the correct tools proper equipment, and thorough training, Most american employers have safety rules, workers are also covered by insurance to pay for injuries on the job.

Edited

_____

_____

_____

_____

_____

Student Assignment

If you are editing a rough draft, check it now for errors in punctuation and capitalization. If you don't have a rough draft, try writing one. Use the prewriting and drafting instructions in Chapters 1–6. Revise for organization (see Chapters 7–12) and style (Chapters 13–18). Edit for fragments and run-on sentences (Chapter 19), subject–verb agreement and consistency of tenses (Chapter 20), pronoun agreement (Chapter 21), and spelling (Chapter 22). Finally, check punctuation and capitalization.

Editing Checklist

After you have edited your rough draft, discuss your writing with your teacher or another person. Use the checklist as a guide.

1. At the end of each sentence, did I correctly use a period, a question mark, or an exclamation point?

2. Within each sentence, did I correctly use commas and apostrophes?

3. Did I capitalize the first letter of the first word in each sentence?

4. Did I correctly capitalize the following: peoples' first and last names and titles, the names of cities, states, and countries, and the names of geographical places?

Video Replay

In the video, Tony supports his son's dream of going to college. Do you have a dream of your future? Write about your dream. How do your friends or your family feel about it? Share your writing with another person.

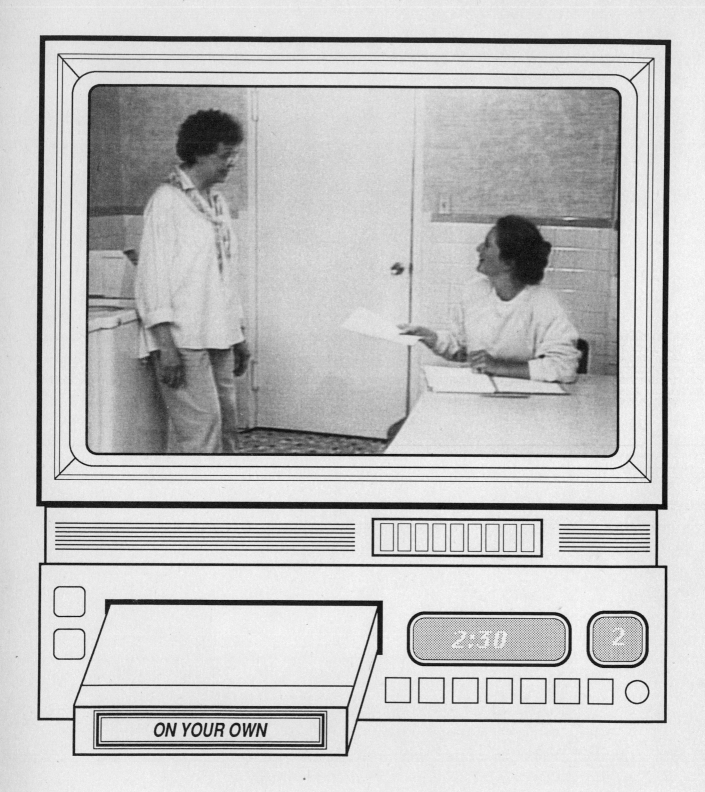

ON YOUR OWN

Taking Pride in Your Writing

VIDEO FOCUS

In the video, Jolene shares letters she has written to a friend and to a new employer with Ms. G. Jolene has rewritten her rough drafts to include all the changes she had made through revising and editing. She is proud of her work.

Sharing writing first with a friend and then with its intended reader is the last stage of the writing process. The readers' reactions help writers discover how clearly they have communicated their intended message.

Chapter Objectives

After seeing the video and completing this chapter, you will understand how to

- prepare a final copy of your writing
- share your writing in many different ways
- publish your writing in several ways.

Key Words

Here are some important words that appear in this chapter or on the video. If you come across a word that is not on this list, write it down and ask your teacher to explain it to you.

publishing	private publishing
illustration	desk-top publishing
demonstration	

Lesson 1 WRITING THE FINAL COPY

Throughout the revising and editing stages, your rough draft probably became very messy. That's normal. A rough draft is supposed to be messy, because it is a working copy.

Now that you have revised and edited your writing, it is time to rewrite the rough draft so that the audience can read the writing easily. Because you want to present your ideas in the best possible form, you need to recopy the final draft.

Here are some suggestions to help you write the final draft.

1. Decide how you want to prepare the final copy. You may handwrite it, type it, or use a computer.

2. Use paper of good quality and a standard size. The standard paper size is 8½ by 11 inches.

3. Leave a margin of one to two inches around all edges of the paper.

4. If you decide to handwrite the final copy, use black or dark blue ink. Be sure your handwriting is easy for someone else to read. If you type the final copy, use a dark ribbon. Work slowly and carefully. If you make a mistake, use correction fluid to cover the error. Be sure that the fluid is dry before you write or type over it.

5. If you decide to use the computer for the final copy, carefully remove the paper from the printer. Then tear off the sides of the computer paper so that no holes appear.

6. Read the final copy aloud to be sure that you have made no new errors. You might want to have another person read the final copy also.

7. If you have written a letter, sign your name clearly. If your letter is a business letter, be sure to include the date and both your address and the address of the business.

Lesson 2 SHARING YOUR WRITING WITH OTHERS, AND PUBLISHING YOUR WRITING

Here are several ways you can share your writing with others.

1. Mailing your personal letter or business letter to the person you have written to is a basic form of sharing your writing which you should practice as often as you can. It will make you check your work carefully, increase your pride in what you do, and give you more confidence in your writing skills.

2. You also can share your personal writings by reading them aloud to a group of other students, to friends who write regularly, or to people who share a special interest with you. If you don't feel comfortable reading aloud, you can just give them copies of your work and talk with them about it later.

3. If your ideas might interest a fairly large number of people, send your writing to the Letters to the Editor section of a newspaper or magazine. For example, many people in your area may be upset about the lateness of city buses. If your writing points out this problem or suggests a solution, the newspaper might print it. Having your writing printed and read aloud by a fairly large audience is called **publishing**.

4. Publish your writing in your employee newsletter. Your coworkers will have the opportunity to learn what you think. You may also encourage them to write something of their own.

5. Read your writing aloud at a meeting. For example, you can read your letter about an unsafe intersection at a meeting of a community council. You can read your humorous description of a coworker when the person is retiring or leaving to take another job. Then you can place the written description in a scrapbook for him or her to enjoy later.

6. You can use pictures to make your writing clear. Such pictures are called **illustration**. You can use photographs, graphs, or drawings. For example, photographs of the damaged vehicle can accompany your written accident report. You can include a graph of the rising cost of utility bills with your letter to the city power commission. If you write to a relative about your child's activities in a daycare center, you can include a drawing by your child, or a snapshot of the child.

7. You can show your readers how to do something that your writing describes. This is called **demonstration**. For example, you can demonstrate how to prepare your favorite recipe on a local TV show. You can mention how the recipe has changed over the years or how you first learned of the recipe. Another way to share a demonstration is to show an employee how to use a new machine, or how to repair a machine, using your written directions as a guide.

8. If you are in a class, you can share your final copy with your classmates by posting it on a bulletin board.

9. If you become very interested in writing and write a lot, you might want to put together some of your work and get it printed by a print shop or a small publisher. Publishing in this way is

called **private publishing**. Small books which look like books produced by publishing companies are now being published on computers. Writing printed in this way is an example of **desk-top publishing**. Someone you know may be able to do desk-top publishing, or know someone who can. Sometimes small bookstores will take copies of desk-top publications and try to sell them for the writer. Many beginning writers start publishing this way. After you have revised them, any of the drafts you have written for the Video Replays, or for the exercise paragraphs, might be printed privately. Such printing would cost some money, so you would need to be serious about publishing to do it. Someone you know, however, might do it very cheaply or even do it free for you.

Student Assignment

Recopy your draft and select the most appropriate way to share it with your reader. Ask your reader to respond to your writing and to your presentation of it.

Sharing

After you have made a final copy of your draft, discuss your writing with your teacher or another person. Use the checklist as a guide.

1. Did I copy my corrected draft neatly and accurately?
2. Am I proud of the appearance of the final copy?
3. Did I choose a satisfying and appropriate way to share my writing with others?
4. Am I proud of the way I have expressed myself in writing?

Video Replay

In the video, Jolene shares a letter of thanks she has written to her new employer. Imagine that you have been hired for a job you really have wanted. Write a letter to someone who helped you get that job, such as a counselor, an employer, a relative, or a friend.

Writing On Your Own

In this book, you have learned the process of writing—from prewriting to writing the rough draft, revising for organization and style, editing, and finally, sharing and publishing.

If you have followed all of the stages of the writing process, your written message should be easily understood by the reader. You can be proud of your ability to communicate clearly in writing.

Remember, writing is an important and powerful way to communicate with other people. By using the writing process, you can convey your ideas successfully to your audience. Use the writing skills presented in this book as much as you can. The more you write, the more confident you will be as a writer, and the more you will enjoy writing.